An Analysis of

Ernest Gellner's

Nations and Nationalism

Dale J. Stahl

Published by Macat International Ltd
24:13 Coda Centre, 189 Munster Road, London SW6 6AW.

Distributed exclusively by Routledge
2 Park Square, Milton Park, Abingdon, Oxon OX14 4RN
711 Third Avenue, New York, NY 10017, USA

Routledge is an imprint of the Taylor & Francis Group, an informa business

Copyright © 2017 by Macat International Ltd
Macat International has asserted its right under the Copyright, Designs and Patents Act
1988 to be identified as the copyright holder of this work.

www.macat.com
info@macat.com

Cataloguing in Publication Data
A catalogue record for this book is available from the British Library.
Library of Congress Cataloguing-in-Publication Data is available upon request.
Cover illustration: Etienne Gilfillan

ISBN 978-1-912302-57-4 (hardback)
ISBN 978-1-912127-30-6 (paperback)
ISBN 978-1-912281-45-9 (e-book)

Notice
The information in this book is designed to orientate readers of the work under analysis,
to elucidate and contextualise its key ideas and themes, and to aid in the development
of critical thinking skills. It is not meant to be used, nor should it be used, as a
substitute for original thinking or in place of original writing or research. References and
notes are provided for informational purposes and their presence does not constitute
endorsement of the information or opinions therein. This book is presented solely for
educational purposes. It is sold on the understanding that the publisher is not engaged
to provide any scholarly advice. The publisher has made every effort to ensure that
this book is accurate and up-to-date, but makes no warranties or representations with
regard to the completeness or reliability of the information it contains. The information
and the opinions provided herein are not guaranteed or warranted to produce particular
results and may not be suitable for students of every ability. The publisher shall not be
liable for any loss, damage or disruption arising from any errors or omissions, or from
the use of this book, including, but not limited to, special, incidental, consequential or
other damages caused, or alleged to have been caused, directly or indirectly, by the
information contained within.

CONTENTS

THE MACAT LIBRARY

The Macat Library is a series of unique academic explorations of seminal works in the humanities and social sciences – books and papers that have had a significant and widely recognised impact on their disciplines. It has been created to serve as much more than just a summary of what lies between the covers of a great book. It illuminates and explores the influences on, ideas of, and impact of that book. Our goal is to offer a learning resource that encourages critical thinking and fosters a better, deeper understanding of important ideas.

Each publication is divided into three Sections: Influences, Ideas, and Impact. Each Section has four Modules. These explore every important facet of the work, and the responses to it.

This Section-Module structure makes a Macat Library book easy to use, but it has another important feature. Because each Macat book is written to the same format, it is possible (and encouraged!) to cross-reference multiple Macat books along the same lines of inquiry or research. This allows the reader to open up interesting interdisciplinary pathways.

To further aid your reading, lists of glossary terms and people mentioned are included at the end of this book (these are indicated by an asterisk [*] throughout) – as well as a list of works cited.

Macat has worked with the University of Cambridge to identify the elements of critical thinking and understand the ways in which six different skills combine to enable effective thinking.
Three allow us to fully understand a problem; three more give us the tools to solve it. Together, these six skills make up the **PACIER** model of critical thinking. They are:

ANALYSIS – understanding how an argument is built
EVALUATION – exploring the strengths and weaknesses of an argument
INTERPRETATION – understanding issues of meaning

CREATIVE THINKING – coming up with new ideas and fresh connections
PROBLEM-SOLVING – producing strong solutions
REASONING – creating strong arguments

To find out more, visit **WWW.MACAT.COM.**

CRITICAL THINKING AND *NATIONS AND NATIONALISM*

Primary critical thinking skill: CREATIVE THINKING
Secondary critical thinking skill: PROBLEM-SOLVING

To the dismay of many commentators – who had hoped the world was evolving into a more tolerant and multicultural community of nations united under the umbrellas of supranational movements like the European Union – the nationalism that was such a potent force in the history of the 20th-century has made a comeback in recent years. Now, more than ever, it seems important to understand what it is, how it works, and why it is so attractive to so many people.

A fine place to start any such exploration is with Ernest Gellner's seminal *Nations and Nationalism*, a ground-breaking study that was the first to flesh out the counter-intuitive – but enormously influential – thesis that modern nationalism has little if anything in common with old-fashioned patriotism or loyalty to one's homeland. Gellner's intensely creative thesis is that the nationalism we know today is actually the product of the 19th-century industrial revolution, which radically reshaped ancient communities, encouraging emigration to cities at the same time as it improved literacy rates and introduced mass education. Gellner connected these three elements in an entirely new way, contrasting developments to the structures of pre-industrial agrarian economies to show why the new nationalism could not have been born in such communities. He was also successful in generating a typology of nationalisms in an attempt to explain why some forms flourished while others fizzled out. His remarkable ability to produce novel explanations for existing evidence marks out *Nations and Nationalism* as one of the most radical, stimulating – and enduringly influential – works of its day.

ABOUT THE AUTHOR OF THE ORIGINAL WORK

Ernest Gellner was born in Paris, France, in 1925. He spent his boyhood in Prague, but his time there ended when Nazi Germany invaded Czechoslovakia and the Jewish Gellners escaped to Great Britain.

Gellner eventually obtained degrees from Oxford and the London School of Economics. Having fled his homeland because of the Nazis' extreme nationalism, it is perhaps not surprising that he came to study the phenomenon. He finally returned to Prague in 1993 as the founding director of the Centre for the Study of Nationalism at the Central European University. He died there just two years later, at the age of 69.

ABOUT THE AUTHOR OF THE ANALYSIS

Dr Dale Stahl holds a doctorate in history from Columbia University. He currently teaches in the College of Liberal Arts and Sciences at the University of Denver, Colorado.

ABOUT MACAT

GREAT WORKS FOR CRITICAL THINKING

Macat is focused on making the ideas of the world's great thinkers accessible and comprehensible to everybody, everywhere, in ways that promote the development of enhanced critical thinking skills.

It works with leading academics from the world's top universities to produce new analyses that focus on the ideas and the impact of the most influential works ever written across a wide variety of academic disciplines. Each of the works that sit at the heart of its growing library is an enduring example of great thinking. But by setting them in context – and looking at the influences that shaped their authors, as well as the responses they provoked – Macat encourages readers to look at these classics and game-changers with fresh eyes. Readers learn to think, engage and challenge their ideas, rather than simply accepting them.

'Macat offers an amazing first-of-its-kind tool for interdisciplinary learning and research. Its focus on works that transformed their disciplines and its rigorous approach, drawing on the world's leading experts and educational institutions, opens up a world-class education to anyone.'

Andreas Schleicher
Director for Education and Skills, Organisation for Economic Co-operation and Development

'Macat is taking on some of the major challenges in university education ... They have drawn together a strong team of active academics who are producing teaching materials that are novel in the breadth of their approach.'

Prof Lord Broers,
former Vice-Chancellor of the University of Cambridge

'The Macat vision is exceptionally exciting. It focuses upon new modes of learning which analyse and explain seminal texts which have profoundly influenced world thinking and so social and economic development. It promotes the kind of critical thinking which is essential for any society and economy. This is the learning of the future.'

Rt Hon Charles Clarke, former UK Secretary of State for Education

'The Macat analyses provide immediate access to the critical conversation surrounding the books that have shaped their respective discipline, which will make them an invaluable resource to all of those, students and teachers, working in the field.'

Professor William Tronzo, University of California at San Diego

WAYS IN TO THE TEXT

KEY POINTS

- Ernest Gellner was a social theorist and anthropologist born in Paris, France, in 1925.
- In *Nations and Nationalism*, published in 1983, he argued that modern industrial society was responsible for the advent of nations.
- *Nations and Nationalism* was the first book to theorize how economic, social, and cultural changes in human society brought about the idea of nation.

Who Was Ernest Gellner?

Ernest Gellner, the author of *Nations and Nationalism* (1983) was born in Paris, France, in December 1925 to parents from Bohemia,* a region of what is today the Czech Republic (then part of the country of Czechoslovakia).* He spent his boyhood in Prague. When Nazi* Germany invaded Czechoslovakia in March 1939, the region became dangerous for Jewish* people. Gellner's family fled to Great Britain. An avid student, Gellner began studying philosophy, politics, and economics at Oxford University's Balliol College in 1943.

World War II* interrupted Gellner's studies. During the last years of the war, he served in a brigade of Czechoslovak expatriates that the British Army organized and armed. He returned to Oxford in 1945, finishing a master's degree with first-class honors, then taught at Oxford and at Edinburgh University for two years. In Edinburgh, he became interested in mountaineering, and he traveled frequently to the Alps* in his later years, sometimes with his students. From 1949 until 1961, Gellner taught sociology* —roughly, the study of the structures and forces that shape and form society—at the London School of Economics. He published his first book, *Words and Things*, in 1959.

After obtaining his doctorate in 1961, Gellner continued teaching at the London School of Economics, now as a professor. Shortly after the publication of *Nations and Nationalism* in 1983, he left London for Cambridge University, where for nine years he taught social anthropology*—a subfield of anthropology (the study of human beings)—often concerned with things such as economics, law, and political organization.

In 1993, the president of the Czech Republic, Václav Havel,* offered Gellner a post at the Central European University. Gellner served as the founding director of its Center for the Study of Nationalism* until his death in 1995 at the age of 69.

What Does *Nations and Nationalism* Say?

Since its publication in 1983, *Nations and Nationalism* has become one of the key texts on the subject of nationalism.* Previously, scholars had believed that nations were ancient and basic—either intrinsic to the human condition or a matter of collective will. Gellner argued instead that nations and nationalism emerged in the modern era.

According to Gellner, before industrialization*—the process by which a society founded on agriculture becomes a society founded on industry, with the profound economic and cultural implications that move brings—societies were culturally differentiated from one another. Large states or empires could rule over diverse populations. It did not matter if the ruling classes spoke a different language or practiced a different religion because people adhered to local customs and traditions that could vary from one region to the next. They belonged to various kinds of groups, but not to nations. Industrialization changed that.

In *Nations and Nationalism,* Gellner argues technological changes and the needs of new industries created a new workforce. To be productive, the workforce required a different set of technical skills. A broad-based education system was born to develop and perpetuate this workforce. As the organization of society required more and more people to share a standard language and culture in order to work effectively, the idea of the nation arose.

Communities coalesced around a unifying culture and, according to Gellner, shared access to this unifying culture and language made a group into "a nation." To administer and protect a national culture, language, and economy, the boundaries of a state had to match those of a culture. States do not necessarily need nations, Gellner says in the text, but nations seek their own states for protection and to perpetuate the national culture and language. From this comes nationalism: a political concept in which state and cultural boundaries match.

This new way of understanding nationalism, as Gellner outlines it in the text, had important implications. First, he argues that the origins of nationalism can be found in the relationship of economy to culture. A nation is neither a fundamental aspect of the human mind nor a deeply embedded facet of human culture. Instead, nations have arisen from historical changes occurring in the modern period.

Second, Gellner shows how a national education system helped create a culture connecting many individuals. In the past, groups with specialized knowledge could function as cultural units. That is, certain groups such as clerics or a financial elite were culturally distinct from the mass of the population. Industrialization changed this, requiring a universal standard of education accessible to all. Gellner refutes the idea that an elite somehow produced nationalism.

Why Does *Nations and Nationalism* Matter?

Nationalism is a slippery subject, something Ernest Gellner knew well. As he wrote, "The idea of a man without a nation seems to impose a … strain on the modern imagination."[1] In *Nations and Nationalism*, Gellner shows how the idea of a nation resulted from a certain set of circumstances. Although nations often try to assert ancient roots, Gellner demonstrates that nations are in fact products of the modern world, born of economic, social, and cultural factors— an idea that refutes many of the myths that nationalists like to tell.

Gellner's book also serves as a reminder that there is nothing "natural" about the nation state. The political legitimacy of the nation state has evolved throughout modern history. *Nations and Nationalism* asks its readers to consider what is true and what is false in the construction of a collective world of nation states.

The importance of *Nations and Nationalism* lies in its documentation of how the nation state came into existence. The text also shows why this concept came to structure human organization and international relations. To understand the history of the modern world, one must understand how the nation originated. More than that, one must understand how nations came to legitimize states. In the past, a right to rule might come from conquest or marriage. Now a state gains and retains legitimacy by protecting the rights of a nation.

More than 30 years after *Nations and Nationalism* first appeared, the concepts it addresses continue to be important—especially in analyzing the power of nationalism and the origin of nations. Cornell University Press republished the book in 2008 and The *Times Literary Supplement* named it one of the 100 most influential books since the end of World War II.

NOTES

1   Ernest Gellner, *Nations and Nationalism* (Oxford: Blackwell, 1983), 6.

SECTION 1
INFLUENCES

MODULE 1
THE AUTHOR AND THE HISTORICAL CONTEXT

KEY POINTS

- *Nations and Nationalism* was one of the first texts to theorize about the modern origins of the nation.

- Gellner loved learning and his training in philosophy* strongly influenced his later work in sociology* (the study of the structure, history, and forces that shape society) and anthropology* (roughly, the study of human beings).

- Gellner's Jewish* upbringing in a country invaded by Nazi* Germany offered him a real-life lesson in the power of nationalism*—the political position that the boundaries of the state and a people's culture should be in agreement.

Why Read This Text?

Ernest Gellner's *Nations and Nationalism*, published in 1983, set forth a deceptively simple idea: nations are a product of the modern world. The nationalist who attributes the origins of the nation to an ancient battle creates a myth to justify the nation's existence. We can trace the real existence and origin of any nation, Gellner argues, to the shift from an agrarian society*—a society with an economy based on farming—to a modern, industrial society.*

In arguing this point in the book, Gellner does not just shift the focus of studies on nationalism. He opens the door to a completely new way of thinking about and researching nationalism. Rather than seeking the origins of the nation in the thoughts of nationalists or in a fundamental aspect of humanness, Gellner shows how the idea

> **&&** At the age of thirteen, Gellner underwent the trauma of that dangerous journey across Europe and lost his friends and social moorings. In his teenage years he dreamed constantly of Prague, viscerally longing to go back. **99**
>
> John A. Hall, *Ernest Gellner: An Intellectual Biography*

of nation connected to the needs of industrial society. According to him, changes in human social organization brought about the idea of nation. Gellner also provides ideas and analytical tools for understanding why nations formed in different places, at different times, and in different ways.

Nations and Nationalism created a framework for thinking about and studying nationalism. Scholars today who work on nationalism or related topics will want to explore and expand on Gellner's ideas—whether they agree or disagree with them.

Author's Life

Ernest Gellner was born in 1925 in Paris, France, to Jewish parents from the Bohemia* region of what was then the country of Czechoslovakia.* With the rise of Adolf Hitler* and the growing power of the racist, nationalistic, and extremely right-wing Nazi party in Germany, Gellner and his family left their home in Prague in 1939 and resettled in Great Britain. An excellent student, Gellner began studying philosophy, politics, and economics at Oxford University's Balliol College in 1943.

World War II* interrupted his studies. During the last years of the war, Gellner served in a brigade of Czechoslovakian expatriates organized and armed by the British Army. To fully grasp *Nations and Nationalism*, it is important to consider Gellner's experience as a Jew forced to flee his home and his decision to fight in another country's military. The rise of Hitler's Nazi Party and the horrific war waged by Hitler's regime demonstrated the power of nationalism to unify peoples in what Gellner saw as "specially virulent" ways.[1] His book is an attempt to understand the origins and conditions of nationalism

Gellner returned to Oxford in 1945, finishing a master's degree with first class honors. From 1949 until 1961, Gellner taught sociology* at the London School of Economics. He also worked on his doctoral dissertation in the field of social anthropology* (roughly, a subfield of anthropology often concerned with things such as customs and political organization), conducting fieldwork in North Africa.

After obtaining his doctorate in 1961, Gellner was made a professor of philosophy and continued teaching at the London School of Economics. In 1984, he left London for Cambridge University and taught social anthropology there for the next nine years. In 1993, he was offered a post in his native Prague at the Central European University, where he served as the founding director of the Center for the Study of Nationalism.*

Gellner died in Prague in 1995 at the age of 69.

Author's Background

One might argue that World War II, which forced Gellner to leave his homeland, changed his scholarly trajectory. He moved away from his early philosophical studies and toward sociology and anthropology. From the 1950s until the time of his death, the main subject underlying his work focused on sociological structures and ways of living in the modern world.*

Questions on such topics led Gellner to his study of the origins and functions of nationalism. His 1964 book, *Thought and Change*, tackled the concept of nationalism, but people outside scholarly circles paid it little attention. Nationalist movements and far-right parties had been discredited as a result of the war. Moreover, the real concern in the immediate decades following World War II was the Cold War*—the growing political and cultural struggle between communist* states and liberal democracies.* This tension simmered until 1991.

In the 1970s, however, a new wave of nationalist sentiment emerged in Europe. As republicans in Northern Ireland sought independence from Great Britain, Ulster Nationalism* was reborn. At the same time, a number of protest movements occurred involving nationalists from the Basque* and Catalan* regions of northern Spain.

The 1970s also saw the rise of a number of far-right political movements throughout Western Europe. In France, a new political party led by Jean-Marie Le Pen* called the "National Front" exploded onto the political scene, proclaiming that Muslim* immigration threatened French identity. Such political struggles over the idea of nation provided the background for a major rethinking of nationalism in academic circles. Ernest Gellner played a significant role in this movement.

NOTES

1   Ernest Gellner, *Nations and Nationalism* (Oxford: Blackwell Publishers, 1983), 139.

MODULE 2
ACADEMIC CONTEXT

KEY POINTS

- Sociology* and anthropology* are both concerned with the behaviors and actions of human communities across time.

- Although both academic disciplines focus on human communities, sociology is generally more interested in large-scale structures and collective behaviors, while anthropology uses qualitative* methods to study smaller groups and interactions.

- Ernest Gellner brought both of these approaches to *Nations and Nationalism*, producing an interdisciplinary book—that is, a book that draws on the aims and methods of more than one academic discipline.

The Work in its Context

Ernest Gellner's *Nations and Nationalism* was published in 1983 as part of a series entitled "Perspectives on the Past," which sought to "discuss problems simply as problems, and not as 'history' or 'politics' or 'economics.'"[1] Gellner's book is purposefully interdisciplinary. He worked with evidence and ideas emanating from several social-science disciplines, including sociology* (the study of social behavior), history,* philosophy,* and social anthropology*—a subfield of anthropology (the study of human beings) that sees human behavior as embedded in social and historical contexts.

That said, Gellner's approach is most informed by ideas within sociology and social anthropology. The academic discipline of sociology coalesced at the turn of the twentieth century under the influence of three different thinkers: the German economist and

> ❝ An outburst of collective emotion in a gathering does not merely express the sum total of what individual feelings share in common, but is something of a very different order ... . It is a product of shared existence, of actions and reactions called into play between the consciousnesses of individuals. If it is echoed in each one of them it is precisely by virtue of the special energy derived from its collective origins. ❞
>
> Emile Durkheim, *The Rules of Sociological Method*

social theorist Karl Marx,* the French sociologist Emile Durkheim,* and the German sociologist Max Weber.* One thing these thinkers had in common is the idea that we can understand human societies by rationally examining certain structures, collective behaviors, or common actions.

The academic discipline of sociology differed from scientific examination of human biology, as well as from psychology's interpretations of individual human consciousness. Unlike these disciplines, sociology pursues knowledge about broad human social phenomena, usually on a quantitative* basis—that is, by measuring data.

Anthropology emerged in the late nineteenth century from practices of natural history*—the study of plants and animals in their environment. European scholars used anthropology as a way to describe faraway, usually colonized, lands and peoples to other Europeans.

Social anthropology combines features of both sociology and anthropology. Like sociology, it focuses on social phenomena such as customs, political organization, family and gender relations, and religion. But it emphasizes qualitative methods—the study of something's qualities—and smaller-scale studies.

Social anthropologists conduct extensive field studies and observations. Like their colleagues in the field of anthropology, they learn native languages and live among their research subjects. In the early twentieth century, historically oriented studies gave way to an emphasis on analyzing contemporary ways of living. Scholars of social anthropology use long-term ethnographic fieldwork*—observation conducted in a specific setting—to describe how people live today.

Overview of the Field

Gellner's work on nationalism* was heavily informed by particular approaches within both sociology and social anthropology. The text reflects the influence of the philosophy of positivism,* which dominated sociology after World War II,*[2] and emphasized the importance that an assertion should be logically or scientifically proven.

Positivism emerged from the writings of the nineteenth-century French thinkers Auguste Comte* and Emile Durkheim. In the mid-nineteenth century, Comte laid the groundwork for the academic discipline that would become sociology. Durkheim, born the year after Comte died, is generally considered one of the primary founders of the discipline.

Durkheim explained his positivist approach in his 1894 book, *The Rules of Sociological Method*. He hypothesized that observation and measurement could reveal certain "social facts."[3] A social fact operated in "general over the whole of a given society whilst having an existence of its own, independent of its individual manifestations."[4] Gellner's investigation of nationalism relies on this insight and method. His text seeks to explain nationalism as more than simply an intellectual exercise. He sees it as a structuring factor in modern society.*

Another approach at the time came from the Polish anthropologist Bronisław Malinowski,* who loomed large within the field of social anthropology—especially the British School,* with its emphasis on long-term observation.

Scholars consider Malinowski the founder of the functionalist* school of anthropology, which theorizes that human beings establish particular institutional mechanisms to satisfy physiological needs[5]— and that we may see cultural practices and attitudes as adaptations to meet these needs. Functionalism in the British school of anthropology was a reaction to the natural history mode of earlier anthropological studies. Those earlier anthropologists saw cultural traits as indications of historical change rather than as being useful in the present.[6]

As part of his functionalist approach, Malinowski claimed that we cannot separate our views of history from the contemporary needs of those attempting to recreate the past. For Malinowski, anthropology aimed to understand why that view existed for a particular individual. In essence, he wanted to "grasp the native's point of view."[7]

Academic Influences

Malinowski's ideas in social anthropology significantly influenced Gellner's understanding of nationalism as a modern phenomenon, For Gellner, Malinowski's ideas helped explain why nationalists project and even invent an ancient history for their nation.

Within sociology, Gellner's positivist approach—his emphasis on logically and scientifically proving assumptions—relates back to Durkheim. In addition, his account of modern society relies on the thought of the German sociologist Max Weber. Weber used the term "disenchantment" to describe features of modern society such as bureaucracy and secularization. He also applied it to knowledge of the world derived from science as opposed to religious belief.[8] Weber argued that modernity* had ushered in an age of disenchantment, and Gellner found that particularly convincing. More specifically, Gellner appropriated Weber's notion of disenchantment when explaining the difference between industrial and pre-industrial societies.

The French sociologist and Cold War* liberal intellectual Raymond Aron* also significantly influenced Gellner. Aron is perhaps best known for his book *The Opium of the Intellectuals* (1955), a critique of French Marxist* theory. In particular, Aron's account of industrialization* specifically influenced Gellner's thinking.

Aron described contemporary economic growth and compared the development of different societies by analyzing a set of hierarchies and national rivalries. He also described the political forms that various societies take: state socialism* (a system in which, for example, industry is not held in private hands), dictatorial regimes (such as that of Nazi* Germany), and liberal democracies (such as those of America and Western Europe, for example).[9] By charting the effects of industrialization, Aron provided fertile ground for Gellner's own analyses.

NOTES

1   R. I. Moore, preface to *Nations and Nationalism* by Ernest Gellner (Oxford: Blackwell Publishers, 1983), viii.

2   George Steinmetz, "American Sociology before and after World War II: The (Temporary) Setting of a Disciplinary Field," in *Sociology in America: A History,* ed. Craig Calhoun (Chicago: University of Chicago Press, 2007), 356–7.

3   Emile Durkheim, *The Rules of Sociological Method*, trans. W. D. Halls (New York: The Free Press, 1982), 52.

4   Durkheim, *Sociological Method*, 59.

5   Ernest Gellner, "The Political Thought of Bronisław Malinowski," *Current Anthropology* 28, no. 4 (1997): 557–9.

6   Michael Young, "Bronislaw Malinowski," in *International Dictionary of Anthropologists*, ed. Christopher Winters (New York: Garland Publishing, 1991), 445.

7   Quoted in Chris Holdsworth, "Bronislaw Malinowski," in *Oxford Bibliographies,* doi: 10.1093/OBO/9780199766567-0096

8   See Max Weber, "Science as a Vocation," in *From Max Weber: Essays in Sociology,* trans. H. H. Gerth and C. Wright Mills (New York: Oxford University Press, 1946), 129–56.

9   See Raymond Aron, *18 Lectures on Industrial Society* (London: Weidenfeld & Nicolson, 1967).

MODULE 3
THE PROBLEM

KEY POINTS

- The idea of "self-determination,"* the process by which a nation takes charge of its own affairs, in the twentieth century provoked scholars to consider how to define a nation and its origins.

- Some scholars saw the ideology* of nationalism* as the product of other ideologies. Others saw it as being produced by a particular form of politics or regime.

- Gellner rejected these stances as inconsistent. He asserted the economic and social basis of nationalism, as well as the role of culture and education in creating a modern nation.

Core Question

Nationalism emerged as a topic of study long before Ernest Gellner wrote *Nations and Nationalism* in 1983. World War I* was set in motion in 1914 by a nationalist act, a Slav* nationalist's assassination of Austrian Archduke Franz Ferdinand.* When the war ended four years later, the Versailles peace negotiations created new "nation states" based on the idea of "self-determination," as championed by US President Woodrow Wilson.*

Wilson based his concept of "self-determination" on the idea that national groups should have the right to found a state and govern themselves. The doctrine raised the hopes of groups around the world that they would be able to create their own internationally recognized states. Clearly, nationalism had reached a new level of political legitimacy. So historians and other scholars

> ❝ Nationalism is primarily a political principle,
> which holds that the political and the national unit
> should be congruent. ❞
>
> Ernest Gellner, *Nations and Nationalism*

set about trying to answer a core question: where did nationalism come from?

In the 1920s and 1930s, scholars began to answer that question. The American Carlton Hayes* and the Prague-born scholar Hans Kohn* were among the most prominent. Both Hayes and Kohn explained nationalism as an ideology—a system of beliefs founded on a desire that a particular world view should be instituted.

For Hayes, nationalism was the product of other ideologies such as liberalism*—a belief emphasizing individual liberty—and imperialism*[1]—the political doctrine of empire building and the dominance of subject people. Kohn, on the other hand, viewed it as a product of certain types of political regimes. Different regimes produced certain types of nationalisms. Kohn divided these into a "Western" liberal and democratic nationalism, and an Eastern nationalism that was "irrational and pre-enlightened."[2] Still, nationalism in his studies was "either reduced to a function of something else (other ideologies, the nation) or … as an incredibly powerful idea that can shape the world in its image."[3]

Another set of scholars of the early twentieth century saw nationalism as grounded in popular political participation enabled by a common language. Leftist intellectuals and politicians such as the Austrian thinker and government minister Otto Bauer* and the statesman Karl Renner* suggested that nationalism had its roots in language and communication.[4] Their ideas, although not as influential in shaping leftist politics, had a longer-lasting impact within the academic world.

The Participants

World War II,* another conflict sparked as a result of nationalist sentiment, left some 60 million people—both military and civilian—dead across Europe, Africa, and Asia. After the war ended, the central question animating scholars remained very much the same as it had been at the end of World War I: what are the origins of nationalism?

But there was another question, too: what factors made nationalism such a powerful force in shaping international politics and history? Gellner brought many of the techniques and insights of sociology* and social anthropology* to his attempts to answer these questions. But he was hardly the only person addressing them.

In 1953, Gellner's fellow social scientist from Prague, Karl Deutsch,* published a book called *Nationalism and Social Communication: An Inquiry into the Foundations of Nationality.* Deutsch's work built on some of the ideas set forth by Otto Bauer.[5] Deutsch collected quantitative* data—that is, measureable data such as statistics—to show how "social communication" affected groups. Good communication between groups helped build affinities, while communication difficulties could present barriers. Some scholars of nationalism, such as the American historian Carlton Hayes, hesitated to embrace Deutsch's theories. But Deutsch's emphasis on communication played a large role in later theories of nationalism.[6]

Another intellectual trend sought to understand the pernicious role of nationalism in the rise and fall of Hitler's* Germany. In 1960, Elie Kedourie,* a Jewish* émigré like Gellner, wrote an essay titled simply "Nationalism." Kedourie wrote of nationalism as a peculiarly European ideology and problem that "had bred fanaticism and irrationalism with truly tragic and pernicious consequences for human society."[7]

In his 1964 book, *Thought and Change*, Gellner resisted Kedourie's characterization. Gellner aligned himself more with Deutsch. He suggested that education, culture, and a shared language were far more important to the power of nationalism than "ideological aberration" or "emotional excess."[8]

The Contemporary Debate

In the early 1980s, when Gellner published *Nations and Nationalism*, several other thinkers brought forward ideas on the same, or a very similar, topic. The scholar most aligned with Gellner's point of view was the British scholar Benedict Anderson.* Anderson published his book, *Imagined Communities: Reflections on the Origin and Spread of Nationalism*, in 1983, the same year as Gellner's work.

Like Gellner, Anderson believed that communication held the key to understanding the origins of nationalism. Anderson advanced the idea of nationalism as "an imagined community." This community depended on a particular configuration of economic and communication technologies, as well as on the weakening of European empires.

Anderson argued that the printing press and the capitalist market that engendered it led to a form of "print-capitalism."* This print-capitalism standardized and consolidated a given language as a consequence of the capitalist* market that produced it—capitalism being the dominant economic, social, and political model in the West and in many other nations in the developing world.

In effect, according to Anderson, reading the same news in the same language helped bring together groups of people into an imagined national community.

The early 1980s also saw the publication of a book by one of Gellner's students, Anthony D. Smith.* Smith took a different view of nationalism from his mentor.[9] In fact, his alternative interpretation of nationalism put him at odds with Gellner's core thesis. Gellner viewed nations and nationalism as entirely modern phenomena. But in his book, *The Ethnic Origins of Nations*, Smith suggested that nations have pre-modern* origins. He argued that we can only comprehend nationalism by looking at its historical ethnic core—and that core has roots going back to long before the modern area.

Smith stated, "Nationalists have a vital role to play in the construction of nations … as political archaeologists rediscovering and reinterpreting the communal past in order to regenerate the community."[10] Gellner, however, rejected Smith's thesis on the ethnic origins of nationalism, viewing it as nothing more than myths created for modern circumstances.[11]

NOTES

1   See Carlton Hayes, *Essays on Nationalism* (New York: The Macmillan Company, 1926).

2   Hans Kohn, *The Idea of Nationalism* (New York: The Macmillan Company, 1944), 457.

3   John Breuilly, *The Oxford Handbook of the History of Nationalism* (Oxford: Oxford University Press, 2013), 4.

4   See Otto Bauer, *The Nationalities Question and Social Democracy,* trans. Joseph O'Donnell (Minneapolis: University of Minnesota Press, 2000). Karl Renner's essay entitled "State and Nation" (1899) has been reproduced in the Bauer translation. Bauer's work was originally published in 1907.

5   Karl Deutsch, *Nationalism and Social Communication: An Inquiry into the Foundations of Nationality* (New York: John Wiley & Sons, Inc., 1953).

6   Carlton J. H. Hayes, "Review of *Nationalism and Social Communication: An Inquiry into the Foundations of Nationality* by Karl Deutsch," *The Catholic Historical Review* 39 (1954): 462–3.

7   Paschalis M. Kitromilides, "Elie Kedourie's Contribution to the Study of Nationalism," *Middle Eastern Studies* 41 (2005): 662. See also Elie Kedourie, *Nationalism* (New York: Praeger, 1960).

8   Ernest Gellner, *Nations and Nationalism* (Oxford: Blackwell Publishers, 1983), 35. See also Brendan O'Leary, "On the Nature of Nationalism: An Appraisal of Ernest Gellner's Writings on Nationalism," *British Journal of Political Science* 27 (1997): 193; and Ernest Gellner, *Thought and Change* (London: Weidenfeld and Nicolson, 1964).

9   Smith carried out his doctoral research under Gellner's supervision at the London School of Economics. Anthony D. Smith, *The Ethnic Origins of Nations* (Oxford: Blackwell, 1986).

10 Anthony D. Smith, "Gastronomy or Geology? The Role of Nationalism in the Reconstruction of Nations," *Nations and Nationalism* 1 (1994): 19.

11 For an account of Smith and Gellner's relationship, see John A. Hall, *Ernest Gellner: An Intellectual Biography* (London: Verso, 2010), 326–7.

THE AUTHOR'S CONTRIBUTION

KEY POINTS

- Ernest Gellner argued that nationalism* resulted from the transformation of agrarian society,* one founded on an agricultural economy, into an industrial society.*

- Gellner was the first to present a theory and argue that nationalism was a modern phenomenon with modern origins.

- While Gellner built on the ideas of earlier scholars about the nature of society, he synthesized them in a novel way.

Author's Aims

In *Nations and Nationalism*, Ernest Gellner aims to prove that nationalism is a unique phenomenon of the modern world*—that is, of the period that began roughly towards the end of the fifteenth century. Gellner argues that nationalism is an unavoidable aspect of modernity, or the modern period. It emerges when agrarian societies became industrialized. Nationalism is not, as many had believed, a primordial facet of human societies. Gellner's contention is that industrialization*—and the processes of urbanization* (people moving from the countryside to the city), bureaucratization* (the building of the procedures and institutions the modern state requires to function), and mass education—made nationalism possible.

These viewpoints required Gellner to describe the process of industrialization and to outline the characteristics of agrarian societies that had not fostered nationalism. In other words, it was not enough to show how industrialization facilitated nationalism; he also had to show why nationalism could not occur within pre-industrial agrarian societies.

> ❝ [A] definition tied to the assumptions of one age (and even then constituting an exaggeration), cannot usefully be used to help to explain the *emergence* of that age. ❞
>
> Ernest Gellner, *Nations and Nationalism*

In the text, Gellner begins with a full explanation of the social, cultural, and economic structures of agrarian societies. Then he undertakes a similar analysis of industrialization. After explaining how industrial development fosters nationalism, Gellner moves on to his broader goal: describing the idea of nation and the characteristics of nationalisms and explaining why certain nationalisms prevailed while others fizzled out. Aiming to provide a "Typology of Nationalisms," as noted in the title of his seventh chapter, Gellner acknowledges and describes in that section how nationalisms differed, even when they emerged from similar societal circumstances and needs.

Approach

Gellner uses an interdisciplinary and speculative approach to the question of the origins of nationalism. He attempts to explain nationalism by placing it within a grand historical narrative. Because *Nations and Nationalism* is a short text—only about 145 pages—Gellner's explanations seem at times schematic (simplified, or making use of diagrams). This is true in both senses of the word: he covers a great deal of history in a short span. And he uses charts and tables to describe large historical processes and societal characteristics.[1]

Gellner's distinction between hunter-gatherer* societies, in which people survive by hunting animals and collecting wild food; agrarian societies, in which social organization is based on an agricultural economy; and industrial societies may be his most original contribution to the study of nationalism. He contends that nationalism could only have emerged in the last of these phases: industrialization.*

To make this argument, Gellner relies on the anthropologist Bronislaw Malinowski's* functionalist* idea, according to which societies create institutions, customs, and culture to meet certain needs.[2] Dividing history between agrarian and industrial societies, Gellner discusses how human societies deal with the pressures of living under particular economic, cultural, and political conditions. In his view, nationalism fulfills social needs caused by industrialization. Having established that nationalism is a key feature of the industrialized world, Gellner examines how the thesis changes our understanding of the world. Viewing nationalism in this way gives us a very different understanding of nations and nationalist movements.

Underlying Gellner's approach is the positivism* of sociology*—the idea that one may become certain of specific "social facts" by observing social activities. Gellner believed he could explain the historical contours of human cultures by observing how their various institutions and practices function. Gellner refused to reduce his sociological analysis of nationalism to a particular idea or value. Instead, in *Nations and Nationalism*, he stresses the deep structural issues involved in society's transition from agrarian to industrial practices. In the last part of the book, he examines the uneven development of these changing societies.

Contribution in Context

Gellner's contribution to the study of nationalism both reacts to and synthesizes several trends. On the one hand, Gellner disputed the view that nationalism emerged from other ideologies or intellectual trends, as the American historian Carlton Hayes* or the British historian Elie Kedourie* proposed.[3] Instead, Gellner sought to produce an account of nationalism that demonstrates its modern origins. He particularly focused on its relationship to industrialization and the collapse of agrarian regimes. For Gellner, scholars who suggest that

MAIN IDEAS

KEY POINTS

- Gellner believed that nationalism* occurred as a result of human social organization, namely the way that different groups within society interact to produce particular culture.

- Nationalism is caused by an adjustment in the relationship between political and economic conditions and human culture, according to Gellner.

- Although Gellner's text ranges widely across time and geography, he strives hard to provide examples and show how his theory operates.

Key Themes

In *Nations and Nationalism*, Ernest Gellner defines nationalism as "a political principle, which holds that the political and the national unit should be congruent"[1]—that is, literally, that they should agree. Gellner's central thesis is that this concept of political legitimacy originates in "a deep adjustment in the relationship between polity and culture" occurring as a result of industrialization.*[2] In other words, the move from an agricultural economy to an industrial economy—industrialization—transforms the organization of society and culture to the point that nationalism becomes a legitimate way of organizing political units.

Gellner's thesis relies on two interlocking interpretations of human social life. The first is the "agrarian"* nature of human societies during the pre-industrial age. Social organization in this phase revolves around a population primarily involved in agricultural work. The various processes that make nationalism a viable and

> ❝ Innovation means doing new things, the boundaries of which cannot be the same as those of the activities they replace.... Nationalism is rooted in a *certain kind* of division of labour, one which is complex and persistently, cumulatively changing. ❞
>
> Ernest Gellner, *Nations and Nationalism*

legitimate "political principle" are not yet present.[3] Gellner's argument here relies on an idea of agrarian society as socially and culturally differentiated. By this he means that the different social strata of agrarian society remain distinct and separate.

The second interpretation has to do with industrial society.* Gellner argues that "the old stability of the social role structure" on which agrarian societies rely cannot survive industrialization. Industrialization changes human societies in several ways. First, it produces the conditions under which nationalism may become an organizing principle. Industrial societies rapidly innovate and "the persistence of occupational change itself becomes the one permanent feature of the social order."[4] This new social order in a modern, industrial society also changes human social roles and works to produce a homogenized culture and language. A sense of unity replaces the social and cultural differentiations that defined agrarian society. In agrarian societies, social loyalties are based on religion or a local potentate. But as society industrializes, it coalesces around the concept of nation.

Exploring the Ideas

Gellner theorized that pre-modern* societies could not support a nationalist organization. This idea depends on a concept of political and cultural difference. According to Gellner, distinctions between human groups function "horizontally." That is, the upper classes of any given pre-modern state may be rigidly separated by culture and language from those they ruled. Examples of such "social dams, separating unequal levels" include a German-speaking Austrian elite or Turkish-speaking Ottoman elite holding sway over a Serbian- or Romanian-speaking population.[5] Gellner argues, "It is clearly advantageous to stress, sharpen and accentuate the ... traits of the privileged groups."[6] The upper classes emphasize their different traits, "endowing them with the aura of inevitability, permanence and naturalness."[7]

In addition to these horizontal divisions, agrarian societies are also vertically differentiated. Agricultural producers are often physically isolated and "inward-turned, tied to the locality by economic need."[8] Local groups have little interest in cultural interconnection. As Gellner notes, they may "have links with a variety of religious rituals, and think in terms of caste, clan, or village (but not of nation) according to circumstance."[9]

For industrialization to function properly, it requires a form of cultural homogeneity* supported by a state. Industrial society operates "on sustained and perpetual growth," which requires a constant input of highly mobile and educated workers.[10] To incorporate such workers into its highly specialized and ever-changing employment roles, an industrial society must produce workers with a high level of basic training. Gellner likens modern society* to an army, which "provides a prolonged and fairly thorough training for all its recruits, insisting on certain shared qualifications."[11]

One of these qualifications is the ability to communicate in technically precise and mutually intelligible language. A "large, indispensable and expensive" education system is the only viable method for achieving these shared qualifications. Education therefore becomes the most important touchstone for "employability, dignity, security and self-respect" and plays a vital role in promoting a particular "school-transmitted culture."[12]

According to Gellner, culture "can no longer be a diversified, locality-tied illiterate little culture or tradition." Instead, the education system must adopt or manufacture a great universal culture. Gellner argues that "the limits of the culture within which [men] were educated are also the limits of the world within which they can, morally and professionally, breathe."[13] Loyalty to a new, shared culture produces "the nation." Nations form when two people "share the same culture" and "recognize certain mutual rights and duties to each other."[14]

Critically—and this is most important to Gellner's argument—the state is the only institution "strong enough to control so important and crucial a function" as sustaining the education system and defending the culture. Gellner argues, this "is the main clue to why state and culture *must* be linked" in the concept of nationalism.[15] The political principle of nationalism flows from this linkage. Since the state is the only viable guarantor of education and thus culture, its borders must encompass all who adhere to the same culture. And there we have the rationale for the nation.

Language and Expression

The Irish academic R. I. Moore,* a specialist in medieval history, asserted that Gellner had produced an "explanation of nationalism … which makes it, for the first time, historically and humanly intelligible."[16] Gellner writes in a clear and lucid style. Not only is the book accessible, at times it is even entertaining.

For example, Gellner invents a group of fictional agriculturalists known as the "Ruritanians" who inhabit the "Empire of Megalomania." The difficulties the Ruritanians face in their attempts to join the dominant Megalomanian culture illustrate important points Gellner wishes to make about the development of the nation.[17]

In trying to provide a clear understanding of nationalism and its effects, Gellner relies on abstractions and hypotheticals. When discussing the problem of minority attributes within larger homogenized populations, he analyzes the hypothetical problems of a group of individuals who are "pigmentationally blue."[18] In most cases, such abstractions help show the general and widespread character and effect of nationalism within his schema.

Still, Gellner's vocabulary can be academic and his arguments, particularly those involving Western philosophy, can be quite complex. This makes the book difficult to negotiate. While college-level students may understand much of the work, they may find some of the philosophical intricacies and historical references puzzling or difficult to assess.

NOTES

1 Ernest Gellner, *Nations and Nationalism* (Oxford: Blackwell Publishers, 1983), 1.

2 Gellner, *Nations and Nationalism*, 35.

3 Gellner notes that, at times, a concept of unity existed in pre-industrial societies, but that this did not attain the level of political principle. Gellner, *Nations and Nationalism*, 14.

4 Gellner, *Nations and Nationalism,* 24.

5 Gellner, *Nations and Nationalism*, 13.

6 Gellner, *Nations and Nationalism,* 11.

7 Gellner, *Nations and Nationalism*, 11.

8 Gellner, *Nations and Nationalism*, 9–10.

9 Gellner, *Nations and Nationalism,* 13.

10 Gellner, *Nations and Nationalism*, 22–3.

11 Gellner, *Nations and Nationalism*, 27–8.

12 Gellner, *Nations and Nationalism*, 36.

13 Gellner, *Nations and Nationalism*, 36.

14 Gellner, *Nations and Nationalism,* 7.

15 Author's emphasis. Gellner, *Nations and Nationalism,* 38.

16 Gellner, *Nations and Nationalism,* viii.

17 Gellner, *Nations and Nationalism*, 58–62.

18 Gellner, *Nations and Nationalism,* 64–5.

SECONDARY IDEAS

KEY POINTS

- Gellner's concept of industrialization* relies on the following ideas: 1) the society is mobile, fluid, and egalitarian, 2) certain human traits prove "resistant" to even dispersal throughout society, and 3) resistant traits form the basis of defining a new nation.

- Gellner uses the idea of resistant traits to distinguish between two stages of nationalism.* These correspond to early or late industrialization.

- Gellner's fascination with different cultures and traits informed his interest in Islam* and his positioning of the religion as having a vital impact on nationalism in Muslim* societies.

Other Ideas

After laying out his central argument in *Nations and Nationalism*, Ernest Gellner introduces two important secondary ideas in explaining nationalism's effects. The first has to do with the effect of industrialization in creating a society that is "random and fluid."[1] Gellner refers to this attribute as "social entropy."*

According to this idea, industrial societies* move toward cultural sameness or homogeneity,* but as they do so, certain human traits prove "entropy-resistant." These are traits that, in a fluid and changing society, cannot become "evenly dispersed."[2] According to Gellner, an entropy-resistant trait "creates fissures, sometimes veritable chasms, in the industrial societies in which it occurs."[3]

Gellner suggests this idea to try to differentiate between two

> **❝** Nationalism is a phenomenon connected not so much with industrialization or modernization as such, but with its uneven diffusion. **❞**
>
> Ernest Gellner, *Thought and Change*

stages of nation making. In early industrialization, the "life chances of the well-off and the starving poor" differ widely. Certain traits of the disadvantaged group could be "entropy-resistant" and thus politically activated. That is, traits not evenly dispersed in society can over time become markers of a certain political status, economic position, or other difference. If so, Gellner argues that individuals may "identify themselves and each other culturally, 'ethnically,'" and a new nation may be born.[4] In the later stages of industrialization, Gellner argues, something different happens: "entropy-resistant" traits that lead to problems of "mobility and equality" will create "national" struggles.[5]

Gellner extends the concept of how nationalisms differ by introducing three other variables: power, education, and culture. According to Gellner, "Modern societies* are always and inevitably centralized, in the sense that the maintenance of order is the task of one agency or group of agencies."[6] Political power in modern societies is thus the domain of a few. Not all members of society can exert power over all other members. People do not always have equal access to education and thus to the national culture. Gellner uses these three variables in a model that shows how only in certain cases will differences result in a national struggle, as opposed to another kind.[7]

Exploring the Ideas

Nationalisms exhibit different characteristics. But Gellner tries to show that they are all fundamentally shaped by cultural differentiation.[*][8] This cultural differentiation may be driven by what he terms "entropy-resistant" traits. Culture is the critical variable in Gellner's typology.[*]

In Gellner's model, while societies may have inequalities in power and education, a national distinction only arises in the face of a cultural difference. For instance, in a society "where a politically weak subgroup is economically or educationally privileged" but shares the same culture as the rest of the society, political conflict may indeed arise—but it will not be due to nationalism.

According to Gellner's scheme, "nationalism is about entry to, participation in, identification with, a literate high culture which is co-extensive with an entire political unit and its total population."[9] A nationalist group will not arise from a previous, larger political unit unless a politically weak group is also cut off from the culture of the powerful. This group may go about identifying and creating its own culture. Using the principle of nationalism, that group may act to create its own state.

Nationalism can also arise when the powerful and powerless share the same culture but are separated into different states. "Unificatory nationalism" may then occur when elements in the different states agitate to unify, becoming part of a single political unit.

Gellner identifies a final form of nationalism: "diaspora[*] nationalism." In this case, a subset of the powerless has both economic and educational opportunity, but it differs culturally from the majority. This can happen in societies where "positions, often too dangerous to be given to locals or full citizens [are] consequently reserved for foreigners."[10] Gellner provides the example of palace guards or "the providers of financial services."[11] With the coming of a "mobile, anonymous, centralized mass society," Gellner argues these services can "hardly be reserved for a minority," and so "the specialized minority groups lose their disabilities [i.e. foreignness], but *also* alas their monopoly and their protection."[12] This leaves the minority group with two choices. It can assimilate to the dominant culture, or it can "create a state of its own, as the new protector of a now un-specialized, generic, newly national culture."[13] Gellner offers the "famous and dramatic case" of Israel as an example of "a successful diaspora nationalism."[14]

Overlooked

The interaction between nationalism and the religion of Islam fascinated Gellner. Religions are often administered by a literate upper class. But in the Industrial Age, Gellner believed that they become secularized, part of a mass national culture.[15] He argues that religion must "throw off its erstwhile legitimating doctrine ... to become the pervasive and universal culture."[16]

Gellner believed that Islam had particular characteristics that allowed it "to survive in the modern world better than do doctrinally more luxuriant faiths."[17] He saw Islam as being without "intellectually offensive frills" and so able to maintain some aspects of its universality and its legitimating influence.[18] It could "legitimate both traditionalist regimes such as Saudi Arabia or Northern Nigeria, and socially radical ones such as Libya, South Yemen or Algeria."[19] Islam could function both to legitimate power and to universalize a particular culture.

Scholars roundly criticized Gellner's stance, and the kernel of his ideas remained unexamined for some time. But John A. Hall,* Gellner's biographer, noted that certain facets of Gellner's analysis of Islam help explain features of political activism in the Middle East.

Hall highlights the Iranian–born scholar Asef Bayat's* 2007 text, *Making Islam Democratic: Social Movements and the Post-Islamic Turn*, a book written 12 years after Gellner's death. Bayat suggests that political and social movements shaped the practice of religion. In Hall's view, this conclusion agrees well with how Gellner viewed the influence of modernity* and nationalism on Islam.[20]

NOTES

1   Ernest Gellner, *Nations and Nationalism* (Oxford: Blackwell Publishers, 1983), 63.

2   Gellner, *Nations and Nationalism*, 64.

3   Gellner, *Nations and Nationalism*, 65.

4   Gellner, *Nations and Nationalism*, 75.

5   Gellner, *Nations and Nationalism*, 75.

6   Gellner, *Nations and Nationalism*, 88.

7   Gellner, *Nations and Nationalism,* 94.

8   Gellner, *Nations and Nationalism*, 96.

9   Gellner, *Nations and Nationalism*, 95.

10 Gellner, *Nations and Nationalism*, 103.

11 Gellner, *Nations and Nationalism*, 103.

12 Gellner, *Nations and Nationalism*, 104.

13 Gellner, *Nations and Nationalism*, 106.

14 Gellner, *Nations and Nationalism*, 106.

15 Gellner, *Nations and Nationalism*, 78.

16 Gellner, *Nations and Nationalism*, 78.

17 Gellner, *Nations and Nationalism,* 80.

18 Gellner, *Nations and Nationalism,* 80.

19 Gellner, *Nations and Nationalism*, 80–81.

20 John A. Hall, *Ernest Gellner: An Intellectual Biography* (London: Verso, 2010), 306. See also Asef Bayat, *Making Islam Democratic: Social Movements and the Post-Islamic Turn* (Stanford: Stanford University Press, 2007).

MODULE 7
ACHIEVEMENT

KEY POINTS

- Gellner's theory of nationalism* redefined much of the thinking on nationalism and refuted four major ideas about the phenomenon.

- While Gellner's ideas were new and important, the slow collapse of the Soviet Union* in the late 1980s brought nationalist groups to the fore and Gellner's work to a broader audience.

- Gellner's work relies on industrialization* to explain how nationalism began in Europe. Critics argue his theory explained more about European history than nationalism in other parts of the world.

Assessing the Argument

Ernest Gellner wrote *Nations and Nationalism* primarily as a work of theory. He evokes a grand narrative of human history to illustrate the modern* origins of nationalism—that is, as having historical roots no older than the end of the fifteenth century, and owing much to the advent of industrialization in the mid-nineteenth century. The work is not a deep historical analysis, and Gellner does not deploy a great deal of data. Instead, the book is almost entirely argumentative.

It is perhaps best, then, to assess Ernest Gellner's theories by noting the many views of nationalism that he rejected. In the penultimate chapter of *Nations and Nationalism*, Gellner reminds his audience of what he considers to be four false theories of nationalism. The first false view suggests that nationalism is "natural and self-evident and self-generating"[1]—that it is somehow fundamental to the human condition.[2]

> **" Nations as a natural, God-given way of classifying men, as an inherent though long-delayed political destiny, are a myth. "**
> Ernest Gellner, *Nations and Nationalism*

The second false position argues that nationalism is "a regrettable accident" and that "political life even in industrial societies could do without it."[3] This view would suggest that no connection whatsoever exists between nationalism and industrialization.

The third perspective involves the Marxist* view of nationalism, founded on the thought of the political theorist Karl Marx.* Gellner calls this "The Wrong Address Theory."[4] In the Marxist reading, societal advancement can only take place through class struggle,* not nationalism. Those who evoke the latter miss the point of revolution.

Finally, Gellner rejects the view that sees nationalism as nothing more than "the re-emergence of the atavistic [that is, ancient and re-emergent] forces of blood and territory."[5] Gellner argues that both those who embrace nationalism and those who reject it endorse this perspective. Those who embrace nationalism view it as a way of renewing the nation's soul. Those who reject it see nationalism as a barbarian movement leading to total disaster.

To Gellner, none of these understandings of nationalism ring true. In his text, he refutes these notions, relying on a complex and compelling argument about social structure. Nationalism could not be supported by agrarian* social organization[6]—that is, the society founded on an agricultural economy—and, therefore, it is not primordial,* or ancient. Nationalism is not an intellectual accident; it emerges from economic and social forces, not the transmission of a particular idea.[7]

To Gellner, the relationship of culture to power remains far more relevant to the rise of nationalism than class struggle or capitalism*—the economic and social system, dominant in the West, in which industry is private and the profits from the labor of working people go to private hands.[8] Finally, Gellner offers an account of needs, or the way industrialization requires a certain social formation. This examination puts to rest the notion that nationalism is simply about blood and territory.[9]

Achievement in Context

Academics generally praised *Nations and Nationalism*, and the text reached a wide readership. In fact, it became Gellner's best-selling work.[10]

Part of the success of *Nations and Nationalism* undoubtedly relates to the timing of its publication. In 1985, Mikhail Gorbachev* came to power as the leader of one of the world's great superpowers, the Soviet Union.* Gorbachev adopted new policies meant to restructure the Soviet economy and government. These policies empowered nationalist movements in Eastern Europe and other areas under Soviet control.

By the late 1980s—just a few years after Gellner's book was published—the Soviet empire had begun to unravel.[11] Its collapse led to the independence of several new states in Eastern Europe, including the Baltic republics of Estonia, Latvia, and Lithuania, and the Ukraine. Several nations in Central Asia and the Caucasus Mountains also gained independence, including large territories such as Kazakhstan, Uzbekistan, and Turkmenistan. The Soviet Union's demise sparked much greater interest in studies of nationalism.

These geopolitical changes had a significant effect on Gellner's career. In the final years of his life—he died in 1995—he traveled a great deal, attending conferences on the subject.[12] He also wrote several new prefaces to the various translations of *Nations and Nationalism* as well as prefatory remarks to other books on the subject. As a prominent and strongly argued text, the book also engendered debate and criticism. Many of Gellner's writings after *Nations and Nationalism* sought to address critics of the book and to fine-tune his argument.[13]

Limitations

Gellner's book offers a well-argued theory of nationalism that may broadly apply to different places and times. Indeed, within a text that runs to fewer than 150 pages, Gellner manages to touch on a remarkable number of subjects. One of Gellner's students noted that he makes "varied staccato comments on multiple issues—the struggles of states over peoples, the reasons for the unlikelihood that Arab nationalism's* defeat would be reversed, the behavior of empires, the mythical character of much nationalist ideology.*"[14]

Gellner's wide-ranging commentary suggests he wanted his work to address many concerns. Cornell University Press published a second edition of *Nations and Nationalism* in 2008, clearly indicating that the book remains relevant almost two decades after its initial publication.

Still, several scholars criticized *Nations and Nationalism*. They saw it as relying too heavily on European history, particularly in its discussion of the development of human societies and its typology* of nationalisms. The Palestinian American intellectual Edward Said* criticized Gellner and the British Marxist historian Eric Hobsbawm* for their "repeated insistence on the *Western* provenance of nationalist philosophies."[15] Gellner's biographer John A. Hall* notes that "it can be said immediately that [Gellner's] theory is marred by only really considering European history."[16] Certain aspects of Gellner's text do seem to rely on a particular European mode of industrialization.

NOTES

1   Ernest Gellner, *Nations and Nationalism* (Oxford: Blackwell Publishers, 1983), 129.

2   This view is often associated with the perspective of the German romantic Johann Gottfried Herder, who argued that the origins of language determine the shape and form of nations. See Johann Gottfried Herder and Michael N. Forster, *Philosophical Writings* (Cambridge: Cambridge University Press, 2002), 65–166.

3   This point of view is most closely associated with Elie Kedourie, *Nationalism* (New York: Praeger, 1960).

4   Gellner, *Nations and Nationalism*, 129.

5   Gellner, *Nations and Nationalism*, 130.

6   Gellner, *Nations and Nationalism*, 8–12.

7   Gellner, *Nations and Nationalism,* 19–38.

8   Gellner, *Nations and Nationalism*, 96.

9   Gellner, *Nations and Nationalism*, 53–5.

10 John A. Hall, *Ernest Gellner: An Intellectual Biography* (London: Verso, 2010), 308.

11 See Robert J. Kaiser, *The Geography of Nationalism in Russia and the USSR* (Princeton: Princeton University Press, 1994).

12 Hall, *Ernest Gellner*, 308.

13 Hall, *Ernest Gellner*, 321.

14 Hall, *Ernest Gellner*, 308.

15 Edward Said, *Culture and Imperialism* (New York: Vintage Books, 1993), 216.

16 Hall, *Ernest Gellner,* 321.

MODULE 8
PLACE IN THE AUTHOR'S WORK

KEY POINTS

- Gellner was a political philosopher. His life's work focused on understanding human societies and culture, though in later life he focused almost solely on nationalism.*

- Gellner viewed *Nations and Nationalism* as the broadest and fullest synthesis of his ideas about society.

- While much of Gellner's theoretical work on Islam* has been roundly criticized, *Nations and Nationalism* has stood the test of time.

Positioning

Nations and Nationalism follows logically from much of Ernest Gellner's early work. The sociological* and social anthropological* concerns on display in *Nations and Nationalism* can be traced to his 1959 book *Words and Things*. In this work, he rejected a theory known as ordinary language philosophy.* Ordinary language philosophy limited philosophy to examining how language works in a given context or community. That is, it held that philosophy should not be concerned with determining what is universally true for all peoples in all societies. Instead, it should focus on how language operates as a system of meaning in a given community.

Gellner believed ordinary language philosophy stripped the discipline of philosophy of any real significance. He argued that it reduced philosophy to nothing more than a descriptive enterprise incapable of offering solutions to the biggest challenges facing the modern world. Five years later, in 1964, he took up one of these challenges, nationalism, in his second published book, *Thought and*

> ❝ *Nations and Nationalism* is at once more sociologically ambitious than *Thought and Change*, bearing the imprint of Gellner's dialogues with Durkheim and Marx; more conceptually novel, displaying the value-added of his theory; and more empirically promising, as it sets out a typology* of nationalism-inducing and nationalism-thwarting situations. ❞
>
> Brendan O'Leary, "On the Nature of Nationalism: An Appraisal of Ernest Gellner's Writings on Nationalism"

Change. This book contains many of the central elements that would later appear in *Nations and Nationalism.* Gellner's interest in, and work on, Islam from the late 1960s until the early 1980s can also be found in *Nations and Nationalism.*[1]

Many of the ideas dominating *Nations and Nationalism* appear in *Thought and Change.* Indeed, chapter 7 offers a glimpse of what is to come in *Nations and Nationalism.* Gellner focuses on a break in human history: the transition from pre-industrial to industrial society.*

As Gellner saw it, this transition radically changed how humans understood their world. Gellner argued in *Thought and Change* that nationalism came into existence as a result of industrialization.* It should not be viewed as a primordial,* or an ancient, notion going back to time immemorial. *Thought and Change* is also where Gellner developed the idea that nationalism must not be conceived of as random. He felt it should be connected with the various institutions and practices of a given state. States work to make nationalism seem "natural" because the concept helps to legitimate their existence.

Integration

Both *Words and Things* (1959) and *Thought and Change* (1964) function more as philosophical rather than anthropological texts. But the latter shows Gellner moving more fully into arguments around the social sciences—namely state formation and the history and effects of industrialization. This trajectory toward social and cultural anthropology grew stronger as Gellner conducted further studies on Islam* and Muslim* societies in North Africa. He published *Saints of the Atlas*, a study of pastoral peoples in Morocco, in 1969. He also published *Muslim Society* in 1981, a book in which he discussed the mechanisms that caused what he viewed as the stability and homogeneity (that is, the internal similarity) of Islamic societies.

While many of the ideas present in *Nations and Nationalism* appeared first in *Thought and Change*, that book did not receive much attention when it was published in the mid-1960s. Gellner's biographer, John A. Hall, notes that, in retrospect, it is clear that *Thought and Change* "foreshadows nearly all his later work," aiming as it did to "provide a social philosophy of modern times."[2] In *Thought and Change*, Gellner addressed what he saw as two interrelated social phenomena: industrialization and nationalism. This exploration set the agenda for the focused study that would later become the most important work of his career, *Nations and Nationalism*.

Significance

Gellner felt *Nations and Nationalism* had fully encapsulated his intellectual views. Shortly after publishing the book, he traveled to Moscow and met a friend, the anthropologist Anatoly Khazanov.* According to Khazanov, Gellner "remarked that the book contained his life."[3]

The book certainly changed his life, garnering huge attention and eventually offering an opportunity for Gellner to leave England and return to his native Prague. He did so at the invitation of Václav Havel,* a Czech dissident and the first democratically elected president of the newly independent Czechoslovakia.* Havel asked Gellner to be the founding director of the Center for the

Study of Nationalism* at the new Central European University. The university had been established just two years earlier, in 1991, after the demise of the Soviet bloc.* The institution's goal was to facilitate cooperation and education among central European nation states. Gellner's decision to leave Cambridge University to join the Central European University gave the institution great credibility.

As director of the Center for the Study of Nationalism, Gellner attracted scholars, diplomats, and policy makers from central Europe and around the world. When Czechoslovakia split into two countries—the Czech Republic and Slovakia—Gellner held conferences and seminars on Czech and Slovakian nationalism aimed at analyzing the political divide between the two countries.

Gellner also turned his attention to other parts of the world. His work on nationalism enabled him to influence public thinking on the situation of formerly dominant minorities in Hungary and Ireland. Gellner used the new research center to discuss a range of topics including Quebec's desire for independence from Canada; the economic, political, and social void created when Russia rejected communism;* and the relationship between Islamic revivalism* and nationalism.[4]

NOTES

1   Ernest Gellner, *Saints of the Atlas* (London: Weidenfeld & Nicolson, 1969) and Ernest Gellner, *Muslim Society* (Cambridge: Cambridge University Press, 1981).

2   John A. Hall, *Ernest Gellner: An Intellectual Biography* (London: Verso, 2010), 131–2.

3   Hall, *Ernest Gellner*, 307.

4   Hall, *Ernest Gellner*, 369.

SECTION 3
IMPACT

THE FIRST RESPONSES

KEY POINTS

- Early criticism of Gellner's *Nations and Nationalism* primarily focused on the relationship he drew between the concepts of industrialization* and nationalism,* as well as the historical examples he deployed to prove his theory.

- Gellner acknowledged the need for more historical evidence, but resisted those who suggested that a social scientist could not identify causal truths in social phenomena—that is, that it was not possible to analyze social behavior in order to identify the causes of those phenomena.

- Gellner's work reshaped the questions one might ask of the origins of nationalism. He found a community willing to grapple with his provocative set of ideas.

Criticism

Ernest Gellner's *Nations and Nationalism* was widely reviewed. The years following its publication in 1983 saw both praise and a number of criticisms of his main arguments.[1]

Several critics denied that a social scientist who stood outside of a given culture could determine how such a society actually operated.[2] Believing such a thing is possible requires accepting that the scientist knows more about the real purpose of values than the people who are in fact practicing them. This is typically understood as functionalism.* John Breuilly,* a professor of nationalism and ethnicity at the London School of Economics, explains that in Gellner's text, "Nationalism is regarded as functional for industrialism ... and its function serves to

> ❝ Instead of arguing that nationalism contradicts capitalism, constitutes an anomaly, or is an emotional, ideological, or intellectual mistake, Gellner states that nationalism was the only possible outcome when industrialism burst into an ethnically differentiated world. ❞
>
> Gale Stokes, "How is Nationalism Related to Capitalism? A Review Article"

explain its existence (teleology*)."[3] In other words, industrialism* requires nationalism—and that means nationalism must exist.

Breuilly found this notion vague because there is no direct cause, arguing, "Industrialism is now less a process of social change underpinning nationalism and more a perceived need which motivates nationalists."[4] The mechanism whereby industrialization propels nationalism is not entirely clear in Breuilly's view. Breuilly feels Gellner has shown a relationship between nationalism and industrialization but not an exact source.

Others criticized Gellner for not providing more specific examples to historically ground what might appear to be a speculative theory on the origins of nationalism. Even so, Gellner's former student Anthony D. Smith* commented, "How far [Gellner's theory] can encompass the some 200 or so nationalisms to date would require more investigation than a general exposition permits." Smith praised Gellner's work as "broadly conceived and stimulating … for without theories to provide perspectives … the manifold researches of individuals becomes disjointed and fragmentary."[5]

Responses

Gellner's biographer, John A. Hall,* notes that "Gellner constantly engaged with his critics."[6] As a consequence, Gellner subtly reworked many of his claims in his later work by describing in detail the different stages in the emergence of nationalism. He also attempted to elaborate on the historical circumstances of nationalism in much of his later work.[7]

Gellner's most direct response to criticism may be found in his aptly titled article "Reply to Critics." Refuting claims that his work is teleological or functionalist, Gellner writes, "Needs engender no realities. But my theory does not sin against this. It is straightforwardly causal."[8] Gellner then recapitulates his argument that, at root, the division of labor* in a society is the mechanism that provokes nationalism.

Some critics charged that his work did not take enough account of history.* Gellner took aim at those who argued it was not possible to use historical interpretation in service of political theory* or who questioned "that genuine knowledge can be independent of the embeddedness of the practitioner in his social position, and that it can be conveyed, learnt and applied through abstract formulation."[9] For Gellner, that viewpoint rejected the very idea of theory and the availability of "objective and articulable knowledge."[10] In repudiating such a stance, Gellner asserted that such criticism granted the critic "privileged access to historical reality, but consigned others to the realm of ideology."*[11] He adamantly refused the idea that his work could not help to explain and order historical developments.

Conflict and Consensus

Gellner's work on nationalism never failed to provoke controversy. Shortly after his death in 1996, a compendium of essays analyzing his ideas was published under the title, *The Social Theory of Ernest Gellner*.[12] In this text, critics leveled more charges against Gellner's theory. The Australian historian Nick Stargardt* argued that industrialization does not necessarily require mass literacy or the standardization of language.[13] He noted that industrialization in Great Britain occurred generations before compulsory education.

Other essays in the book suggested that people in many major industrial cities speak a variety of native languages, which possibly undermines Gellner's claim about the relationship between industry and a homogenous, or internally similar, culture* and language.[14]

More interestingly, a number of critics argued no relationship necessarily existed between industrialization and nationalism. They suggested nationalism may arise even in the absence of an industrial society.* For example, nationalism occurred in colonial India, but its leading proponent, Mahatma Gandhi,* explicitly rejected Western industrialization.[15] As this collection of critical essays demonstrated, many of the charges leveled at the book when it was published in the 1980s remained relevant years later.

The rise of other theories brought new kinds of scrutiny to Gellner's work. For example, postcolonial theory* sought to analyze and destabilize the modes of thought that support Western colonialism* and imperialism.* Encompassing several academic disciplines, it removed European narratives from their formerly central place in scholarly conversation and added a new focus on the histories of peoples in other parts of the globe. The use and interpretation of history remained at the center of Gellner's battles with proponents of postcolonial theory, particularly the scholar Edward Said.*

Newer works on nationalism by postcolonial theorists, such as those by the Indian scholar Partha Chatterjee* in the 1990s, have offered alternative interpretations of nationalism in non-European contexts. They have also questioned whether Gellner's theories apply to the world outside of Europe.[16]

NOTES

1 For a bibliography detailing a list of Gellner's critics see: John A. Hall, *Ernest Gellner: An Intellectual Biography* (London: Verso, 2010), 321–8.

2 John Breuilly, introduction to Ernest Gellner, *Nations and Nationalism* (Oxford: Blackwell Publishers, 1983), XL–XLII.

3 John Breuilly, "Reflections on Nationalism," *Philosophy of the Social Sciences* 15 (1985): 68.

4 Breuilly, "Reflections," 68.

5 Anthony Smith, "Review of *Nations and Nationalism* by Ernest Gellner," *Millennium: Journal of International Studies* 12 (1983): 281.

6 John A. Hall, *Ernest Gellner: An Intellectual Biography* (London: Verso, 2010), 326.

7 John Breuilly, introduction to *Nations and Nationalism: New Perspectives on the Past*, by Ernest Gellner (Ithaca, NY: Cornell University Press, 2nd Edition, 2008), XXX–LIII.

8 Gellner, "Reply to Critics," *New Left Review* I/221: 84.

9 Gellner, "Reply to Critics," 88.

10 Gellner, "Reply to Critics," 89.

11 Gellner, "Reply to Critics," 89.

12 John A. Hall and Ian Charles Jarvie, eds., *The Social Philosophy of Ernest Gellner* (Amsterdam: Rodopi, 1996).

13 Nick Stargardt, "Gellner's Nationalism: The Spirit of Modernism," in *The Social Philosophy of Ernest Gellner*, eds. John A. Hall and Ian Jarvie (Atlanta: Rodopi, 1996), 171–89.

14 Breuilly, introduction to *Nations and Nationalism*, XXXV–XXXVII.

15 Breuilly, introduction to *Nations and Nationalism*, XXXIX.

16 See Partha Chatterjee, *The Nation and Its Fragments: Colonial and Postcolonial Histories* (Princeton: Princeton University Press, 1993) and particularly *Nationalist Thought and the Colonial World: A Derivative Discourse* (London: Zed Books, 1996), 21–2.

MODULE 10
THE EVOLVING DEBATE

KEY POINTS

- Gellner worked in the years after publication of *Nations and Nationalism* to add additional historical evidence and expand his theory.

- Although a "Gellner school" did not emerge from *Nations and Nationalism*, the text remained a touchstone for further research and debate.

- Gellner's resistance to postcolonial theory,* which critically analyzes the legacies of the modes of thought on which Western colonialism* and imperialism were founded, provoked an ongoing debate about the relationship of culture to power and how best to analyze it.

Uses and Problems

Ernest Gellner carried forward many of his ideas years after the publication of *Nations and Nationalism*. In particular, he responded to critiques by publishing two additional texts. Both *Encounters with Nationalism* in 1994 and the posthumously published *Nationalism* (1997) added to his basic theory in substantive ways. In this last book, Gellner "put forward a new way of classifying nationalism,* largely overlapping with the previous typology.*"[1]

Gellner's new concept divided the history of nationalism into stages and geographic zones. Both the zones and the historical examples that he cites focus almost entirely on Europe, bypassing the charge that Gellner's theory is inapplicable to other regions.[2] Gellner did make a significant revision to his discussion of Islam.* He included the Muslim world as one of his "zones." Instead of

> **❝ It is nationalism which engenders nations, and not the other way round. ❞**
> Ernest Gellner, *Nations and Nationalism*

arguing that Islam would facilitate nationalism, Gellner argued that the religion "emerged as the dominant and victorious trend" over nationalism.[3]

Gellner's views on Islam raised the ire of the Palestinian American postcolonial theorist* Edward Said.* Said suggested that Gellner's perspective was potentially driven by ideology*—that, in fact, it was indistinguishable from Western imperialism.* Said argued that Gellner's work on Islam presupposed Western standards of truth and reason, which led Gellner to a biased and prejudiced understanding of Islamic societies.[4]

In a now-famous battle in the pages of the *Times Literary Supplement*, Gellner and Said traded barbs. The spat began when Gellner reviewed Said's book *Culture and Imperialism*, in which Said criticized Gellner's views on nationalism. Writing of "Orientalism,"* Said's argument that in the European colonial imagination the civilizations east of Europe were exotic and uncivilized, with certain implications that endure in many forms of Western culture, Gellner said that Said was "inventing a bogy called Orientalism" and that "the problem of power and culture … is too important to be left to [literary criticism]."[5] Said replied that "the generalities which he adduces to my argument are his, not mine." He accused Gellner of being ignorant about both Muslim* societies and Orientalism.[6] Gellner's reaction sought to characterize Said's idea of Orientalism "as the attribution of superior merit and truth in virtue of *who* one is … rather than to the affirmations themselves on merit."[7]

While the argument continued through several more published letters, the essential difference between the two men involves their interpretation of the motives of history. For Gellner, grand historical forces set in motion Western imperialism and nationalism, a "transformation of the world by a new technology, economy and science."[8] For Said, imperialism was also a cultural project, which explains his emphasis on those who "represent the historical experience of decolonization."[*9]

Both Gellner and Said are interested in the relationship of power to culture. But they fundamentally disagreed on the mechanisms that shape history.

Schools of Thought

Despite the success of *Nations and Nationalism,* Gellner never established a particular school of thought. Nevertheless a number of his students advanced the field of nationalist studies. Gellner's students rearticulated many of his ideas while also rejecting some of his fundamental claims.

Anthony D. Smith* may be Gellner's best-known former student. He argued against one of Gellner's basic points, namely that nationalism is an entirely modern* form of myth-making (that is, its roots are no older than, roughly, the late fifteenth century). Smith agreed with Gellner that nationalism's emergence is inseparable from modern industrialization. However, he argued that nations have pre-modern* ethnic origins.[10]

Another important student of Gellner's is John A. Hall,* who recently completed a well-received biography of Gellner.[11] Hall acknowledges that Geller influenced his own work on nationalism, but fundamental differences between them remain. In particular, Hall criticizes Gellner for his lack of engagement with politics. In Hall's view, that does not mean Gellner's theory of nationalism is useless, but rather that it must be completed.[12]

Brendan O'Leary* was a student of Gellner's who later came to believe that much of what Gellner wrote on nationalism was either wrong or no longer applicable. O'Leary accepted Gellner's novel claim that nationalism is linked to industrialization.* Yet he saw Gellner's focus on industrialization as too reductive.[13] O'Leary instead argued that political causes not connected to industrialization might be the primary factors for the rise of nationalism.[14]

In Current Scholarship

Scholars in various fields study nationalism, and *Nations and Nationalism* takes an interdisciplinary approach to the subject. So scholars from many different disciplines have some involvement with Gellner's work, and many have appropriated Gellner's ideas to update them. The sociologist* Michael Mann* embraces Gellner's overall theory of nationalism, for example, but has expanded it by linking it to European military history, colonization,* and the exploitation of workers.[15] The political scientist* Michael Lessnoff,* meanwhile, has complicated Gellner's account of Islam and modernity* by arguing that different intellectual trends provided the pathway into modernity for Islam.[16]

Although influenced by Gellner's thought, the British anthropologist* Alan Macfarlane* has argued that Gellner's theory of nationalism fails to provide an adequate account of European civil society and how trust was developed within such societies.[17] The political scientist Mark Haugaard* has attempted to enrich Gellner's understanding of nationalism by exploring how power operated in pre-modern* and modern European society. In this sense Haugaard attempts to reconcile Gellner's work on industrialization with social theorist Michel Foucault's* understanding of power.[18]

The sociologist Nicos Mouzelis* has worked to update Gellner's concept of modernity by arguing that the transition from agrarian society* to industrial society* only became possible once the political sphere dominated the economic sphere. This would resolve the criticism that nationalism in Gellner's argument depends too much on industrialization and not enough on the political transformations that Europe experienced during the modern era.[19] And, as we have seen, Edward Said condemned *Nations and Nationalism* as inherently imperialist. All of these writers can be seen as working with Gellner's thought, however, rather than explicitly against it.

NOTES

1   John A. Hall, *Ernest Gellner: An Intellectual Biography* (London: Verso, 2010), 321.

2   Hall, *Ernest Gellner,* 323–4.

3   Ernest Gellner, *Nations and Nationalism* (Oxford: Blackwell Publishers, 1983), 83.

4   See Edward W. Said and Gauri Viswanathan, *Power, Politics and Culture: Interviews with Edward W. Said* (New York, NY: Pantheon Books, 2001), 297.

5   Ernest Gellner, "The Mightier Pen?," review of *Culture and Imperialism* by Edward Said, *The Times Literary Supplement,* February 19, 1993, 2–3.

6   Edward Said, Letter to Editor, *Times Literary Supplement*, March 19, 1993.

7   Ernest Gellner, Letter to Editor, *Times Literary Supplement*, April 9, 1993.

8   Gellner, "The Mightier Pen?," 2.

9   Edward Said, Letter to Editor.

10   See Anthony D. Smith, *The Ethnic Origins of Nations* (Oxford: Blackwell, 1986).

11   Hall, *Ernest Gellner.*

12   Hall, *Ernest Gellner*, 334–7.

13   Brendan O'Leary, "Ernest Gellner's Diagnoses of Nationalism: A Critical Overview, or, What is Living and What is Dead in Ernest Gellner's Philosophy of Nationalism," in *The State of the Nation: Ernest Gellner and the Theory of Nationalism*, ed. John A. Hall (Cambridge: Cambridge University Press, 1998), 40–90.

14   Brendan O'Leary, "On the Nature of Nationalism: An Appraisal of Ernest Gellner's Writings on Nationalism," *British Journal of Political Science* 27 (1997): 204.

15 Michael Mann, "Predation and Production in European Imperialism," in *Ernest Gellner and Contemporary Social Thought*, eds. Sinisa Malesevic and Mark Haugaard (Cambridge: Cambridge University Press, 2007), 50–74.

16 Michael Lessnoff, "Islam, Modernity and Science," in *Ernest Gellner and Contemporary Social Thought*, 189–226.

17 Alan Macfarlane, "Ernest Gellner on Liberty and Modernity," in *Ernest Gellner and Contemporary Social Thought*, 31–49.

18 Mark Haugaard, "Power, Modernity and Liberal Democracy," in *Ernest Gellner and Contemporary Social Thought*, 75–104.

19 Nicos Mouzelis, "Nationalism: Restructuring Gellner's Theory," in *Ernest Gellner and Contemporary Social Thought*, 125–39.

MODULE 11
IMPACT AND INFLUENCE TODAY

KEY POINTS

- *Nations and Nationalism* continues to inform and fertilize debates about the nation and nationalism,* as seen with the publication of a new edition in 2008.
- The way Gellner positioned Islam within his work still attracts significant criticism from major thinkers.
- Further work on nationalism acknowledges Gellner's major ideas, often noting ways to open up new avenues of inquiry.

Position

Although certain aspects of Ernest Gellner's *Nations and Nationalism,* originally published in 1983, may seem dated, the book remains a seminal text in the field of nationalism studies. It is essential reading for contemporary scholars approaching the question of nationalism. Cornell University Press published a new edition of the text in 2008, and the book has been translated into 24 languages and sold more than 160,000 copies—an unusually high number for an academic work.

Indeed, *Nations and Nationalism* continues to receive considerable scholarly attention. Two edited volumes have recently appeared that discuss Gellner's work on nationalism at length. *The State of the Nation: Ernest Gellner and the Theory of Nationalism,* edited by John A. Hall and published in 1998,[1] raises criticisms of Gellner's work, but it also attempts to revise and update it for the contemporary context. In 2007, an anthology, *Ernest Gellner and Contemporary Social Thought,* brought together students of Gellner and outside scholars to reassess his work.[2]

> **❝ [What] remains of Gellner's thought after these various critiques? Arguably what is most impressive is that, ten years after his death, his research problematic —the questions he raised and the way he answered them—is still at the cutting edge of social theory. ❞**
> Mark Haugaard and Sinisa Malesevic, "Introduction: An Intellectual Rebel with a Cause"

Gellner's fundamental insight and distinct contribution to the discipline remains the connection he made between industrialization* and nationalism. Scholars disagree with many elements of his thought, but even today critics conclude that Gellner was right to connect nationalism with modern industrialization. In a 2007 article with the subtitle, "Should we still read Ernest Gellner?," the Spanish historian Daniele Conversi* responded with a resounding, "Yes." Conversi's article expands on Gellner's theory of cultural homogenization* and notes that "Gellner was among the first scholars to theorise its linkage with nationalism as a consequence of industrialization."[3]

Interaction

Many more-recent works have found inspiration in Gellner's *Nations and Nationalism*, even as their authors have taken issue with different aspects of his explanation.

In the 1990s, the Canadian academic Charles Taylor* attempted to use many of Gellner's insights by adding a political dimension.[4] He hoped to explain why nationalism had taken on such significant meaning for large numbers of people and how this had influenced their political actions. Taylor applied these reformulations to Québécois nationalism.[5]

The comparative literature professor Gregory Jusdanis*

wrote *The Necessary Nation* (2001) on the place of culture in nation-making. In it, he commented that "Gellner explains the conspicuousness of culture in nation building," even as he "does not really explain why inherently a modern, industrial society must be a secular nation state."[6]

The historian Tara Zahra* acknowledged a debt to Gellner's thesis in her examination of "national indifference" among Czech and German-speakers in the region of Bohemia* in her 2008 book, *Kidnapped Souls: National Indifference and the Battle for Children in the Bohemian Lands, 1900–1948*. But she also noted that "nations may be modern, but nationalization did not unfold through an organic and inevitable process of modernization."*[7]

Even scholars working on different topics have used Gellner's understanding of nationalism. In his 2002 book examining ethnic violence, the political scientist* Roger Petersen* discussed Gellner's hypothetical "Ruritarians" and their choice of a "nationalist option." But Petersen noted that "Gellner, operating at a historical/structural level and interested in nationalism as a broad phenomenon, is not particularly inclined to specify the force or mechanisms that so 'impelled' the Ruritarians."[8]

The Continuing Debate
Some would argue that Gellner's biggest impact in the past 15 years has stemmed from his writing about the shape and form of Muslim* societies. After the terrorist attacks on the United States sponsored by al-Qaeda* on September 11, 2001, public interest in Islam* increased dramatically. Six years after Gellner's death, the postcolonial* theorist Edward Said* criticized the news media for turning to the ideas of scholars such as Gellner and Bernard Lewis* in an attempt to understand Muslim societies and beliefs.[9] Said accused the news media of "being prone to welcome, I would say it is primed for, Gellner's theses that [Muslims'] culture and

politics can be discussed in thousands of words without a single reference to people, periods, or events."[10]

The Pakistani American anthropologist Talal Asad* has criticized Gellner along the same lines, saying Gellner's conception of Islamic* society involves "the definition of Muslim history as the 'mirror image' … of Christian* history, in which the connection between religion and power is simply reversed."[11] Asad has argued that Gellner uses too many Western presuppositions that do not adequately represent Muslim values and practices.

The social theorist Partha Chatterjee* represents another influential strand of present-day thinking on nations and nationalism. Chatterjee's work has taken issue with both Gellner's thesis and that of his contemporary Benedict Anderson.* Chatterjee, whose largest problem with such accounts of nationalism has been that the idea of modernity* is not effectively interrogated, has commented, "History, it would seem, has decreed that we in the postcolonial world shall only be perpetual consumers of modernity."[12] According to Chatterjee, Gellner's version of nationalism produces a "modular" notion of history,* a model that is simply exported to transform other parts of the globe. In reducing history to this modular form, the agency, attitudes, and activities of local populations matter little.

NOTES

1   John A. Hall, ed., *The State of the Nation: Ernest Gellner and the Theory of Nationalism* (Cambridge: Cambridge University Press, 1998).

2   Sinisa Malesevic and Mark Haugaard, eds., *Ernest Gellner and Contemporary Social Thought* (Cambridge: Cambridge University Press, 2007).

3   Daniele Conversi, "Homogenisation, Nationalism and War: should we still read Ernest Gellner?," *Nations and Nationalism* 13 (2007): 387–8.

4   Charles Taylor, "Nationalism and Modernity," in *The State of the Nation: Ernest Gellner and the Theory of Nationalism*, ed. John A. Hall (Cambridge: Cambridge University Press, 1998), 169–90.

5   Charles Taylor, "The Politics of Recognition," in *Multiculturalism: Examining the Politics of Recognition,* ed. Amy Gutmann (Princeton, NJ: Princeton University Press, 1994), 25–74.

6   Gregory Jusdanis, *The Necessary Nation* (Princeton: Princeton University Press, 2001), 62–3.

7   Tara Zahra, *Kidnapped Souls: National Indifference and the Battle for Children in the Bohemian Lands, 1900–1948* (Ithaca: Cornell University Press, 2008), 6.

8   Roger Petersen, *Understanding Ethnic Violence: Fear, Hatred, and Resentment in Twentieth-Century Eastern Europe* (Cambridge: Cambridge University Press, 2002), 57.

9   See, for instance, Bernard Lewis, "The Roots of Muslim Rage," *The Atlantic,* September 1990, 47–60.

10 Edward Said and Gauri Viswanathan, *Power, Politics, and Culture: Interviews with Edward W. Said* (New York, NY: Pantheon Books, 2001), 297.

11 Talal Asad, *The Idea of an Anthropology of Islam*, Occasional Papers Series (Washington, DC: Georgetown University Center for Contemporary Arab Studies, 1986), 5. See also Talal Asad, *Genealogies of Religion: Discipline and Reasons of Power in Christianity and Islam* (Baltimore, MD: Johns Hopkins University Press, 1993).

12 Partha Chatterjee, *The Nation and Its Fragments* (Princeton: Princeton University Press, 1993), 5.

MODULE 12
WHERE NEXT?

KEY POINTS

- As one of the most influential books published since the end of World War II, *Nations and Nationalism* may find new life as globalization* and international alliances suggest a redefinition of the nation state.

- Gellner's work was seminal in its discovery of nationalism's* origins in modernity* and industrial society,* and it will probably serve as a point of reference for further questions and research.

- *Nations and Nationalism* has added significantly to understanding of the relationship of culture and power in the creation of the nation.

Potential

One cannot overstate the influence of Ernest Gellner's *Nations and Nationalism*. In 2008, the *Times Literary Supplement* named it one of the 100 most influential books since World War II.[*1] It is likely to continue to be a text that scholars must wrestle with, acknowledge, expand upon, and criticize. Nationalism continues as a force in today's societies. It shapes both individual identities and relations between people.

Some nation states in the contemporary world are relatively young. Countries such as the United Arab Emirates (UAE), founded in 1971, include diverse populations from different parts of the globe. But the UAE offers very limited paths to citizenship. In such countries, the state supports events and programs designed to invent, encourage, and educate people about a particular national vision

> **❝** Not much real comfort for our woes is on offer ... What Gellner offered was something more mature and demanding: cold intellectual honesty. **❞**
>
> John A. Hall, *Ernest Gellner: An Intellectual Biography*

of "heritage."[2] Future scholars may debate whether Gellner's thesis applies to such places, even as young countries grow and change.

Gellner's work may have continued relevance in judging the importance of nationalism as a force shaping relations between people. Some have suggested that globalization—the increasing trend towards cultural and economic integration across the globe—will cause the decline of the nation state.[3] This raises a number of questions. If free-market economic policies appear to threaten national identities, will there be a nationalist backlash? If globalization serves as a culturally homogenizing* force, what will the role and reaction of carefully constructed national cultures be? Gellner's thoughts on nationalism can help provide answers.

Future Directions

At the heart of Gellner's work is the idea that the destabilizing forces of industrialism* cause nationalism to take a certain shape in a given society. Industrialization* changes existing social structures, and national ideas often take root during that period of change. Gellner's student John A. Hall* has attempted to reconcile Gellner's work on nationalism with the expanding phenomenon of globalization. Hall aims to examine "the viability of the nation state in the face of contemporary economic forces."[4] He understands nationalism as a modern* phenomenon connected to economic forces, an idea that originated with Gellner. Hall analyzes how new changes in these economic forces may now affect nations and nationalism.

Meanwhile, scholars such as the Turkish-born scholar of genocide

Ugur Umit Ungor* and the American historians David Ludden,* Tara Zahra,* Timothy Snyder,* and Francine Hirsch,* among many others, continue to clarify the process of nation making and nationalism in particular historical cases.[5] Their work grapples with various theories of nationalism, of which Ernest Gellner's may be the most prominent. Each of these authors tries to show historically how the shift from multicultural empires to nation states happened at various scales. Many, including Hall, continue to work directly with Gellner's texts. But Gellner's innovations have informed and opened up a much larger sphere of intellectual inquiry for scholars in different disciplines to pursue.

Summary

Ernest Gellner's *Nations and Nationalism* offers a readable and innovative account of the origin of two important phenomena: 1) the nation, and 2) the idea of the nation, generally called nationalism. Gellner's book was the first to make a clear argument about the connection between nationalism and the modern world. He theorized that nations formed as a result of the social and cultural changes brought on by industrialization.

Gellner's book has stood the test of time because of its sophistication and the clarity of his model. His text does a great deal of conceptual work. He connects significant changes in the economy—specifically, industrialization—to the modern state, education, culture, and power. Because of the work's broad range and the causal links Gellner draws between these concepts, *Nations and Nationalism* has inspired many readers. It has also invited much criticism and provided countless avenues of new research for scholars in a number of academic disciplines.

Economic forces, technology, science, and culture continue to change the world, so Gellner's theory continues to receive attention. It may even gain new relevance. Questions about globalization, migration, and war, in particular, all test Gellner's ideas about the links between economic development, cultural homogeneity, and the power of the state. The book will continue to provoke comments and questions well into the twenty-first century.

NOTES

1   *Times Literary Supplement*, "The Hundred Most Influential Books Since the War," October 1995.

2   For recent work on nationalism and citizenship in the United Arab Emirates, see Ahmed Kanna, *Dubai: The City as Corporation* (Minneapolis: University of Minnesota Press, 2011) and Neha Vora, *Impossible Citizens: Dubai's Indian Diaspora* (Durham: Duke University Press, 2013).

3   See for instance Martin Wolf, "Will the Nation-State Survive Globalization?," *Foreign Affairs* 80 (2001): 178–90.

4   John A. Hall, "Globalization and Nationalism," *Thesis Eleven* 63 (2000): 67.

5   David Ludden, *Contesting the Nation: Religion, Community, and the Politics of Democracy in India* (Philadelphia: University of Pennsylvania Press, 1996); Ugur Umit Ungor, *The Making of Modern Turkey: Nation and State in Eastern Anatolia, 1913–1950* (London: Oxford University Press, 2012); Tara Zahra, *Kidnapped Souls: National Indifference and the Battle for Children in the Bohemian Lands, 1900–1948* (Ithaca: Cornell University Press, 2008); Timothy Snyder, *The Reconstruction of Nations: Poland, Ukraine, Lithuania, Belarus, 1569–1999* (New Haven: Yale University Press, 2003); and Francine Hirsch, *Empire of Nations: Ethnographic Knowledge and the Making of the Soviet Union* (Ithaca: Cornell University Press, 2014).

GLOSSARIES

GLOSSARY OF TERMS

Agrarian society: a society that depends on an economy centered on the cultivation and trade of agricultural products.

Al-Qaeda: a militant group that employs an extreme interpretation of Islam to justify its actions. Osama bin Laden and several other militants founded the group sometime in the late 1980s.

Alps: a mountain chain in Europe extending from France in the west to Austria in the east.

Anthropology: the scientific study of human beings and culture.

Arab nationalism: the belief that Arabic-speaking peoples share a common heritage and should be part of a single nation state.

Basque: an ethnic group occupying a region known as the Basque Country, which is located in an area of modern-day Spain and France stretching from the western Pyrenees Mountains to the coast of the Bay of Biscay.

Bohemia: a region in what is today the western half of the Czech Republic. It was once a province of Austria-Hungary and, after that, a part of Czechoslovakia.

British School of Anthropology: a particular school of thought in social anthropology associated with Bronislaw Malinowski. It sought to break free from historical interpretation to analysis of contemporary societies through long-term ethnographic fieldwork.

Bureaucratization: the creation of procedures, protocols, and institutions (bureaucracy) necessary to the functioning of the modern state.

Capitalism: an economic system in which property and capital goods are privately owned and economic production aims to make a profit.

Catalan: an ethnic group and language of northeastern Spain. It is the national and official language of the tiny state of Andorra in the Pyrenees Mountains.

Center for the Study of Nationalism: a research center established in 1993 at the Central European University in Prague. Ernest Gellner was the center's first director.

Christian: an adherent of the religion of Christianity.

Christianity: a religion of over 2 billion adherents founded in the first century B.C.E. Its believers consider Jesus of Nazareth to be the son of God and the Messiah prophesied in the Old Testament of the Bible.

Class struggle: competing socioeconomic classes entering into conflict. Karl Marx believed that class struggle was the means to make radical changes in society.

Cold War: a period of high political tension, from roughly 1947 to 1991, between a group of countries known as the Western bloc that included the United States and its European allies, and the Soviet bloc, a group of nations that included the Soviet Union and its European allies.

Colonialism: the policy of one country obtaining control over the territory of another by means of settling its own people to populate and govern the new territory.

Communism: a political theory and economic ideology derived from the writings of Karl Marx that advocates the collective ownership of property and social revolution ending in a classless society.

Cultural differentiation: distinctions made between different human groups on the basis of real or perceived cultural characteristics.

Cultural homogenization: the reduction of cultural diversity, usually accomplished through the invention, popularization, or diffusion of cultural concepts and symbols.

Czechoslovakia: a state in eastern Central Europe formed in 1918 as a result of the peace treaty ending World War I. It was peacefully dissolved in 1993 into two separate states, the Czech Republic and Slovakia.

Decolonization: the overturning of colonial control in a state that has been dependent on an outside power. Decolonization may be understood, in a political sense, as attaining independence and, in a cultural sense, as the removal of colonial social and cultural effects.

Diaspora: the forced dissemination of a people or culture from its place of origin or ancestral homeland.

Division of labor: on a general level, the apportionment of tasks in a society to different individuals. Karl Marx made a distinction between the economic division of labor (a result of technical needs) and the social division of labor (achieved through social hierarchies).

Ethnographic fieldwork: a method of social-science research used to describe the modes of everyday life of a particular group. "Fieldwork" refers to long-term observation of subjects in a particular setting or place.

Functionalism: the method of studying, or the theory of, the functional interactions and adaptations of particular phenomena within a given framework or structure.

Globalization: the process whereby the world becomes more interconnected. Such interconnectedness takes many forms—including economic, political, and cultural ones—and is often seen as negatively affecting national identity.

History: the branch of human knowledge involved with studying and analyzing past events. Historians produce narratives of these events, usually attempting to discern the causes of change over time and thus producing histories.

Hunter-gatherer society: a society made up of people who are reliant on hunting, fishing, and the harvesting of wild foodstuffs.

Ideology: a system of beliefs founded on a desire that a particular world view should be instituted.

Imperialism: a system of rule based on concepts of dominion and superiority whereby one society dominates the territory—as well as the political, social, and economic life—of another society.

Industrial society: see Industrialism and Industrialization.

Industrialism: a series of economic and social changes brought about by a shift in energy use by human populations. New energy sources, such as water and steam power, made it possible to develop new machines and manufacturing processes. It began in England in the eighteenth century and later spread to Western Europe and the United States.

Industrialization: the process of transformation from an economy based on agriculture to the manufacture of goods, resulting in a very different socioeconomic order.

Islam: one of the great monotheistic—the belief in one god who is transcendent over creation—religions that emerged from the Middle East. Founded in the early seventh century in what is today western Saudi Arabia, Islam has spread around the globe to now include over 1.5 billion followers, known as Muslims.

Islamic revivalism: a movement to return to the fundamental tenets of the religion of Islam. Modern revivalists may trace their roots to Egyptian and South Asian activists of the late nineteenth and early twentieth centuries.

Jew: an adherent of the religion of Judaism.

Judaism: a monotheistic—the belief in one god who is transcendent over creation—religion that began 3,500 years ago in what is now known as the Middle East. The prophet Moses founded the religion. Its most important scriptural text is the Torah, the five books of Moses.

Liberal democracy: a system of government in which all eligible members of the population participate, usually through elected representatives.

Liberalism: a political philosophy most associated with seventeenth-century British philosopher John Locke. Locke argued that human beings have a natural right to life, liberty, and property, which government must not transgress.

Marxism: a school of social and economic thought derived from the ideas of Karl Marx and Friedrich Engels that influenced the development of the socialist and communist movements. Its key ideas are based around class struggle, the overthrow of the bourgeoisie by the proletariat, and the replacement of a capitalist system with socialism.

Modern society: see Modernity.

Modern world: see Modernity.

Modernity: the modern period, beginning around the end of the fifteenth century, when advances in science drove many changes in technology, warfare, politics, and exploration. In the study of history, the modern period generally coincides with the increasing predominance of Europe on the world stage as a result of industrialization and globalization.

Modernization: a concept that seeks to identify the steps or parameters necessary for less-developed societies to attain the same level of social and economic progress as developed societies.

Muslim: an adherent of the religion of Islam.

Nationalism: "a political principle, which holds that the political and the national unit should be congruent," according to Gellner. Nationalism has many forms and meanings; it is used, for example, to refer to extreme patriotism or to a nation's desire for self-determination.

Natural History: a study of organisms, including plants and animals, in their environment. Before the twentieth century, natural history often also included observations and studies of non-European peoples.

Nazism: the policies and practices under the dictatorship of the Austrian-born German politician Adolf Hitler (1889–1945) as leader of the Nazi Party and, later, Führer (1934–45). It was a totalitarian regime characterized by genocidal anti-Semitism, state control of the economy, and national expansion.

Ordinary language philosophy: a concept that limited philosophy's aim to examining how language works in a given context or community. It held that philosophy should not be concerned with determining what is universally true for all peoples in all societies, but should instead focus on how language operates as a system of meaning in a given community.

Orientalism: a term used for the imitation or depiction of cultures predominant in areas east of Europe. Edward Said's formulation of the term refers to the patronizing frame of many Western depictions, which he argued stripped the subject culture of dynamism and diversity.

Philosophy: the academic field focused on fundamental problems of mind, language, existence, and reason. The word comes from the ancient Greek for "love of wisdom."

Political realism: a theory that national self-interest drives foreign policy. When diplomacy fails, national self-interest could result in conflict between two nations.

Political science: the social-science academic discipline most concerned with the study of political activities, government, and political behavior. Political scientists may use quantitative or qualitative methods in their attempts to understand the underlying factors that affect how politics works.

Political theory: the study of the ideas and concepts at work in the understanding and evaluation of politics.

Positivism: the idea that any rational assertion can be verified, either by scientific methods or a logical proof.

Postcolonial theory: the study of Western colonialism and imperialism's cultural and political legacy. It is not defined as part of a particular academic field but it typically involves such disciplines as literature and anthropology.

Pre-modern: the period in history prior to the modern period, meaning the era preceding the late fifteenth century when changes in technology and science led to increasing globalization and industrialization.

Primordial: a term used to denote something as existing from the very beginning, as essential or original.

Print-capitalism: the consolidation and standardization of a language as a consequence of the printing press and the capitalist market that engendered it.

Qualitative: methods of research based on the analysis of the subject's particular qualities.

Quantative: methods of research based on the measurement of data such as statistics.

Self-determination: a political principle that a people who consider themselves a nation should have the right to form a state and govern themselves.

Slav: an ethno-linguistic group occupying much of the eastern half of Europe.

Social anthropology: a subfield of the academic discipline of anthropology that combines features of both sociology and anthropology. Like sociology, it focuses on social phenomena such as customs, political organization, family and gender relations, and religion. But it emphasizes qualitative methods, or the study of something's qualities, and smaller-scale studies. Social anthropologists emphasize fieldwork as they pursue questions related to human interaction, including social customs, patterns of exchange, family structures, political organization, and religion. The subfield generally views culture as embedded in social and historical contexts.

Social entropy: regarding social systems, this is the idea that social structures or networks have a tendency to break down over time. This can lead to the disappearance of social distinctions.

Socialism: an economic and social system in which the free market is regulated for the sake of social justice and economic equality.

Sociology: the academic discipline focused on studying collective social behaviors usually using not only quantitative methods, but also qualitative research techniques. Sociologists focus on a broad range of subjects including culture, religion, social class, institutions, gender, law, and sexuality.

Soviet bloc: the communist states of Eastern Europe, including the Balkans, which shared a common ideology during the Cold War, which lasted from the end of World War II to the collapse of the Soviet communist system (1947–91).

Soviet Union, or USSR: a kind of "super state" that existed from 1922 to 1991 and centered primarily on Russia and its neighbors in Eastern Europe and the northern half of Asia. It was the communist pole of the Cold War, with the United States as its main "rival."

Teleology: literally means the purpose of something, but in many contexts refers to determining the reason something exists or acts by virtue of what it appears to do or exist for.

Typology: a system for classifying things according to type, or study of how things have similar traits or characteristics.

Ulster Nationalism: the concept that the northeastern part of the island of Ireland, currently a part of the United Kingdom, should become its own separate country and not join the Republic of Ireland, which occupies the rest of the island.

Urbanization: the movement of population from rural areas to urban centers and the attendant social, political, and economic effects.

World War I: a global conflict that began in 1914, pitting the Allies, a group of countries including the United Kingdom, France, and Russia (and eventually the United States) against the Central Powers, which included Germany, Austria-Hungary, and the Ottoman Empire. The war ended in 1918 with the defeat of the Central Powers.

World War II: a European conflict between Germany and its neighbors that began in 1939 and eventually resulted in the eruption of tensions around the world. The United States entered the conflict in 1941. The war ended with the defeat of Germany and her allies and the dropping of atomic weapons on Hiroshima and Nagasaki in Japan. Close to 60 million people—about two-thirds of them civilians—died before the war was brought to an end.

PEOPLE MENTIONED IN THE TEXT

Benedict Anderson (b. 1936) is a contemporary British scholar best known for his 1983 book, *Imagined Communities: Reflections on the Origin and Spread of Nationalism*, in which he systematically describes the emergence of nationalism in the world during the past three centuries.

Raymond Aron (1905–83) was a French sociologist and Cold War champion of liberalism perhaps best known for his 2001 book, *The Opium of the Intellectuals*, which argued that Marxism is not a scientific philosophy but a secularized religion.

Talal Asad (b. 1932) is an anthropologist who teaches at the City University of New York. He is best known for his work on the anthropology of Western secularism and the concept of religion.

Otto Bauer (1881–1938) was one of the leading left-wing thinkers in Vienna, Austria. He held a PhD in law and served as the foreign minister of Austria from 1918–19 at the end of World War I.

Asef Bayat is a sociologist who teaches at the University of Illinois at Urbana-Champaign. He specializes in the study of social movements, urban life, and Islam in the Middle East.

John Breuilly (b. 1946) is professor of nationalism at the London School of Economics and has written extensively on the subject of nationalism and ethnicity.

Partha Chatterjee (b. 1947) is a professor of anthropology and South Asian studies at Columbia University. His work focuses on empire and nationalism in South Asia.

Auguste Comte (1798–1857) was a French philosopher who helped found the discipline of sociology and the concept of positivism.

Daniele Conversi is a research professor at the University of the Basque Country in Bilbao, Spain. He focuses on the history of nationalism and cultural homogenization.

Karl Deutsch (1912–92) was born to a German-speaking family in Prague and went on to obtain two doctorates—one in political science and the other in sociology. He worked extensively on nationalism, international relations, and cybernetics.

Emile Durkheim (1858–1917) is generally considered the founder of the French sociological tradition. He is best known for his works on religion, suicide, and the division of labor.

Franz Ferdinand (1863–1914) was an archduke of Austria and heir to the throne of the Austro-Hungarian Empire. His assassination prompted Austria-Hungary to declare war against Serbia, which led to the outbreak of World War I.

Michel Foucault (1926–84) was a French philosopher and social theorist. He is best known for his works on the relationship between power, institutions, and knowledge.

Mohandas K. (Mahatma) Gandhi (1869–1948) was the leader of the Indian independence movement against the rule of the British Empire. Gandhi employed nonviolent techniques of civil disobedience to resist British rule.

Mikhail Gorbachev (b. 1931) was the last general secretary of the Soviet Union, appointed in 1985. His economic and political reforms helped to end the Cold War, but they also resulted in the collapse of the Soviet bloc.

John A. Hall (b. 1949) is a professor of sociology at McGill University in Montreal, Canada. He obtained his PhD from the London School of Economics and has written extensively on nationalism and the life and ideas of Ernest Gellner.

Mark Haugaard (b. 1961) is a professor of political science at the National University of Ireland Galway. His research interests focus on political and sociological theory.

Václav Havel (1936–2011) was a writer and political dissident of Czech origin. After the overthrow of Czechoslovakia's communist government, Havel became the country's president. When Czechoslovakia split into two countries—the Czech Republic and Slovakia—Havel became the first president of the new Czech Republic, a post he held for 10 years from 1993 to 2003.

Carlton J. H. Hayes (1882–1964) was an American historian of nationalism and a diplomat. He served as the president of the American Historical Association and was appointed the American Ambassador to Spain during World War II.

Johann Gottfried Herder (1744–1803) was a German philosopher perhaps best known for his writings on the origins of human language and German nationalism.

Francine Hirsch (b. 1967) is professor of history at the University of Wisconsin-Madison. She specializes in Russian and Soviet history.

Adolf Hitler (1889–1945) was the leader of the Nazi party in Germany. Elected chancellor of Germany in 1933, he became a dictator and styled himself the Führer from 1934 until his suicide in 1945. Under Hitler's leadership, the German military invaded several neighboring countries, starting World War II. His policies also resulted in the systematic genocide of nearly 6 million Jews, homosexuals, ethnic minorities, and other citizens considered "undesirable."

Eric Hobsbawm (1917–2012) was a British Marxist historian considered by many to be the greatest British historian of the twentieth century. He is perhaps best known for his five-volume work on the history of modern Europe.

Gregory Jusdanis (b. 1955) is professor of classics at Ohio State University. His research focuses on aesthetics, nationalism, and cultural studies.

Elie Kedourie (1926–92) was a British historian of the Middle East. Of Iraqi Jewish background, Kedourie wrote extensively on empire, Middle East politics, and nationalism.

Anatoly Khazanov (b. 1937) is the Ernest Gellner Professor of Anthropology at the University of Wisconsin-Madison. His work focuses on nomadic pastoralists, nationalism and ethnicity, and collective memory.

Hans Kohn (1891–1971) was an American philosopher and historian. He is known for his work on nationalism in Eastern Europe.

Jean-Marie Le Pen (b. 1928) is a French conservative and nationalist politician. In 1972 he helped to found the French party, Front National (also known as the National Front). The party's platform calls for legislation to curtail immigration and France's return to its old currency, the franc, instead of the euro.

Michael Lessnoff (b. 1940) is a research fellow in political science at the University of Glasgow. His research focuses on the emergence of modernity.

Bernard Lewis (b. 1916) is a British American historian of Islam, best known for his 2002 book, *What Went Wrong?: Western Impact and Middle Eastern Response*, which provides a number of speculative answers as to why the Muslim world fell behind advances made by European societies during the modern period.

David Ludden (b. 1948) is professor of history at New York University. He has written extensively on agricultural communities on the Indian subcontinent.

Alan Macfarlane (b. 1941) is a British anthropologist who has written many historical works on England, Nepal, Japan, and China.

Bronisław Malinowski (1884–1942) was a Polish-born British anthropologist who argued that anthropologists should participate in their studies. This is known as the technique of the participant observer.

Michael Mann (b. 1942) is a British sociologist teaching at the University of California at Los Angeles. His work focuses on state power and bureaucratization in the twentieth century.

Karl Marx (1818–83) was a German economist and political theorist who became the founder of modern communism. He co-wrote *The Communist Manifesto* (1848) with the industrialist Friedrich Engels and authored *Capital* (1867).

R. I. Moore (b. 1941) is a professor and specialist in medieval history. He has written several works on the concept of heresy.

Nicos Mouzelis (b. 1939) is professor of sociology at the London School of Economics. His research focuses on the sociology of development.

Brendan O'Leary (b. 1958) is a political scientist teaching at the University of Pennsylvania. His research focuses on nationalism, democracy, and constitutional design.

Roger Petersen is a political scientist who teaches at the Massachusetts Institute of Technology. His research centers on comparative politics with an emphasis on conflict and violence.

John Plamenatz (1912–75) was a political philosopher. He is best known for his work on democracy and spent most of his career at the University of Oxford.

Karl Renner (1870–1950) was an Austrian politician and first chancellor of the Austrian Republic after World War I. His academic work focused on law and property. He worked with Otto Bauer on ideas of legal protection of minority groups.

Edward Said (1935–2003) was a Palestinian American literary theorist and advocate for Palestinian rights, best known for his book *Orientalism* (1978), which argues that Orientalist scholarship is inextricably tied to the imperialist societies that produce it.

Anthony D. Smith (b. 1933) is a British ethnographer and sociologist, currently a professor emeritus at the London School of Economics. Smith's work on nationalism argued that nations have pre-modern origins.

Timothy Snyder (b. 1969) is a professor of history at Yale University. His work focuses on the history of Eastern and Central Europe and the history of the Holocaust.

Nicholas Stargardt (b. 1962) is an Australia-born historian and fellow at Oxford University's Magdalen College. His research focuses on modern European history.

Charles Taylor (b. 1931) is a Canadian philosopher best known for his work on Hegel, modern understandings of selfhood, and the history of secularization in Europe and North America.

Ugur Umit Ungor (b. 1980) is a historian and sociologist at Utrecht University. His research focuses on mass violence and genocide.

Max Weber (1864–1920) was a German sociologist famous for his work on economy and society, notably his 1905 book, *The Protestant Ethic and the Spirit of Capitalism.*

Woodrow Wilson (1856–1924) was the 28th president of the United States. Wilson served from 1913 to 1921 and his administration supervised America's entry into World War I. He is perhaps best known for his Fourteen Points speech to the American Congress on January 8, 1918, which called for "a general association of nations" and led to the establishment of the League of Nations (an international organization founded in January 1920 after the end of World War I to help settle international disputes and which was dissolved in 1946).

Tara Zahra is professor of history at the University of Chicago. Her research centers on family, nation, and ethnicity in Europe during the twentieth century.

WORKS CITED

WORKS CITED

Anderson, Benedict R. O'G. *Imagined Communities: Reflections on the Origin and Spread of Nationalism.* London: Verso, 1983.

Aron, Raymond. *18 Lectures on Industrial Society. The Nature of Human Society.* London: Weidenfeld & Nicolson, 1967.

Asad, Talal. *Genealogies of Religion: Discipline and Reasons of Power in Christianity and Islam.* Baltimore, MD: Johns Hopkins University Press, 1993.

____. *The Idea of an Anthropology of Islam.* Occasional Papers Series. Washington, DC: Georgetown University Center for Contemporary Arab Studies, 1986.

Bauer, Otto. *The Nationalities Question and Social Democracy.* Translated by Joseph O'Donnell. Minneapolis: University of Minnesota Press, 2000.

Bayat, Asef. *Making Islam Democratic: Social Movements and the Post-Islamic Turn.* Stanford: Stanford University Press, 2007.

Breuilly, John. Introduction to *Nations and Nationalism: New Perspectives on the Past*, by Ernest Gellner. 2nd ed. Ithaca, NY: Cornell University Press, 2008.

____. *The Oxford Handbook of the History of Nationalism.* Oxford: Oxford University Press, 2013.

Chatterjee, Partha. *The Nation and Its Fragments.* Princeton: Princeton University Press, 1993.

____. *Nationalist Thought and the Colonial World: A Derivative Discourse.* London: Zed Books, 1996.

Conversi, Daniele. "Homogenisation, Nationalism and War: Should We Still Read Ernest Gellner?" *Nations and Nationalism* 13, no. 3 (2007): 371–94.

Deutsch, Karl. *Nationalism and Social Communication: An Inquiry into the Foundations of Nationality.* New York: John Wiley & Sons, Inc., 1953.

Durkheim, Emile. *The Rules of Sociological Method.* Translated by W. D. Halls. New York: The Free Press, 1982.

Gellner, Ernest. *Words and Things: A Critical Account of Linguistic Philosophy and a Study in Ideology.* Boston, MA: Beacon Press, 1959.

____. *Thought and Change.* The Nature of Human Society Series. London: Weidenfeld and Nicolson, 1964.

____. *Saints of the Atlas.* The Nature of Human Society Series. London: Weidenfeld & Nicolson, 1969.

____. *Muslim Society*. Cambridge Studies in Social Anthropology. Cambridge; New York, NY: Cambridge University Press, 1981.

____. "The Mightier Pen?" Review of *Culture and Imperialism* by Edward Said. *The Times Literary Supplement,* February 19, 1993, 2–3.

____. *Encounters with Nationalism*. Oxford; Cambridge, MA: Blackwell, 1994.

____. *Nationalism*. New York, NY: New York University Press, 1997.

____. "The Political Thought of Bronisław Malinowski." *Current Anthropology* 28, no. 4 (1997): 557–9.

____. "Reply to Critics." *New Left Review* 221, no. 1 (1997): 81–118.

____. *Nations and Nationalism: New Perspectives on the Past*. 2nd ed. Ithaca, NY: Cornell University Press, 2008.

Hall, John A. *Ernest Gellner: An Intellectual Biography*. London; New York, NY: Verso, 2010.

____. "Gellner's Metaphysics." In *Ernest Gellner and Contemporary Social Thought*, edited by Sinisa Malesevic and Mark Haugaard, 253–70. Cambridge: Cambridge University Press, 2007.

____. "Globalization and Nationalism." *Thesis Eleven* 63 (2000): 67

Hall, John A., ed. *The State of the Nation: Ernest Gellner and the Theory of Nationalism*. Cambridge: Cambridge University Press, 1998.

Hall, John A. and Ian Charles Jarvie, eds. *The Social Philosophy of Ernest Gellner.* Amsterdam: Rodopi, 1996.

Hastings, Adrian. *The Construction of Nationhood: Ethnicity, Religion, and Nationalism.* The 1996 Wiles Lectures Given at the Queen's University of Belfast. Cambridge: Cambridge University Press, 1997.

Haugaard, Mark. "Power, Modernity and Liberal Democracy." In *Ernest Gellner and Contemporary Social Thought*, edited by Sinisa Malesevic and Mark Haugaard, 75–104. Cambridge: Cambridge University Press, 2007.

Hayes, Carlton J. H. *Essays on Nationalism.* New York: The Macmillan Company, 1926.

____. "Review of *Nationalism and Social Communication: An Inquiry into the Foundations of Nationality* by Karl Deutsch." *The Catholic Historical Review* 39 (1954): 462–3.

Herder, Johann Gottfried and Michael N. Forster. *Philosophical Writings*. Cambridge Texts in the History of Philosophy. Cambridge: Cambridge University Press, 2002.

Hirsch, Francine. *Empire of Nations: Ethnographic Knowledge and the Making of the Soviet Union*. Ithaca: Cornell University Press, 2014.

Hobsbawm, E. J. *Nations and Nationalism Since 1780: Programme, Myth, Reality*. 2nd ed. Cambridge: Cambridge University Press, 1992.

Hobsbawm, E. J., and T. O. Ranger. *The Invention of Tradition.* Past and Present Publications. Cambridge: Cambridge University Press, 1984.

"The Hundred Most Influential Books since the War." *Times Literary Supplement,* October 1995.

Holdsworth, Chris. "Bronislaw Malinowski." In *Oxford Bibliographies.* Accessed June 19, 2015. doi: 10.1093/OBO/9780199766567-0096.

Jusdanis, Gregory. *The Necessary Nation.* Princeton: Princeton University Press, 2001.

Kanna, Ahmed. *Dubai: The City as Corporation.* Minneapolis: University of Minnesota Press, 2011.

Kaiser, Robert J. *The Geography of Nationalism in Russia and the USSR.* Princeton: Princeton University Press, 1994.

Kedourie, Elie. *Nationalism*. 4th ed. Oxford: Blackwell, 1993.

Kitromilides, Paschalis M. "Elie Kedourie's Contribution to the Study of Nationalism." *Middle Eastern Studies* 41 (2005): 661–3.

Kohn, Hans. *The Idea of Nationalism*. New York: The Macmillan Company, 1944.

Lessnoff, Michael. "Islam, Modernity and Science." In *Ernest Gellner and Contemporary Social Thought*, edited by Sinisa Malesevic and Mark Haugaard, 189–226. Cambridge: Cambridge University Press, 2007.

Lewis, Bernard. "The Roots of Muslim Rage." *The Atlantic,* September 1990, 47–60.

Ludden, David. *Contesting the Nation: Religion, Community, and the Politics of Democracy in India*. Philadelphia: University of Pennsylvania Press, 1996.

Macfarlane, Alan. "Ernest Gellner on Liberty and Modernity." In *Ernest Gellner and Contemporary Social Thought*, edited by Sinisa Malesevic and Mark Haugaard, 31–49. Cambridge: Cambridge University Press, 2007.

Malesevic, Sinisa, and Mark Haugaard, eds. *Ernest Gellner and Contemporary Social Thought.* Cambridge: Cambridge University Press, 2007.

Malinowski, Bronislaw. *A Scientific Theory of Culture and Other Essays* Chapel Hill: University of North Carolina Press, 1944.

Mann, Michael. "Predation and Production in European Imperialism." In *Ernest*

Gellner and Contemporary Social Thought, edited by Sinisa Malesevic and Mark Haugaard, 50–74. Cambridge: Cambridge University Press, 2007.

Moore, R.I. Preface to *Nations and Nationalism*, by Ernest Gellner, vii–viii. Oxford: Blackwell Publishers, 1983.

Mouzelis, Nicos. "Nationalism: Restructuring Gellner's Theory." In *Ernest Gellner and Contemporary Social Thought*, edited by Sinisa Malesevic and Mark Haugaard, 125–39. Cambridge: Cambridge University Press, 2007.

O'Leary, Brendan. "Ernest Gellner's Diagnoses of Nationalism: A Critical Overview, or, What Is Living and What Is Dead in Ernest Gellner's Philosophy of Nationalism." In *The State of the Nation: Ernest Gellner and the Theory of Nationalism*, edited by John A. Hall. Cambridge: Cambridge University Press, 1998.

____. "On the Nature of Nationalism: An Appraisal of Ernest Gellner's Writings on Nationalism." *British Journal of Political Science* 27 (1997): 191–222.

Petersen, Roger. *Understanding Ethnic Violence: Fear, Hatred, and Resentment in Twentieth-Century Eastern Europe.* Cambridge: Cambridge University Press, 2002.

Plamenatz, John. "Two Types of Nationalism." In *Nationalism: The Nature and Evolution of an Idea*, edited by Eugene Kamenka, 22–36. London: Edward Arnold, 1976.

Said, Edward W. *Orientalism*. New York, NY: Pantheon Books, 1978.

____. *Culture and Imperialism.* New York: Vintage Books, 1993.

Said, Edward W. and Gauri Viswanathan. *Power, Politics, and Culture: Interviews with Edward W. Said*. New York, NY: Pantheon Books, 2001.

Smith, Anthony D. "Review of *Nations and Nationalism* by Ernest Gellner." *Millennium: Journal of International Studies* 12 (1983): 280–82

____. *The Ethnic Origins of Nations*. Oxford: Basil Blackwell, 1986.

____."Gastronomy or Geology? The Role of Nationalism in the Reconstruction of Nations." *Nations and Nationalism* 1 (1994): 3–23.

Snyder, Timothy. *The Reconstruction of Nations: Poland, Ukraine, Lithuania, Belarus, 1569–1999.* New Haven: Yale University Press, 2003.

Stargardt, Nick. "Gellner's Nationalism: The Spirit of Modernism." In *The Social Philosophy of Ernest Gellner*, edited by John A. Hall and Ian Jarvic, 171–89. Atlanta, GA: Rodopi, 1996.

Steinmetz, George. "American Sociology before and after World War II: The (Temporary) Setting of a Disciplinary Field." In *Sociology in America: A History,* edited by Craig Calhoun, 314–66. Chicago: University of Chicago Press, 2007.

Taylor, Charles. "The Politics of Recognition." In *Multiculturalism: Examining the Politics of Recognition*, edited by Amy Gutmann. Princeton, NJ: Princeton University Press, 1994.

____. "Nationalism and Modernity." In *The State of the Nation: Ernest Gellner and the Theory of Nationalism*, edited by John A. Hall, 191–218. Cambridge: Cambridge University Press, 1998.

Ungor, Ugur Umit. *The Making of Modern Turkey: Nation and State in Eastern Anatolia, 1913–1950.* London: Oxford University Press, 2012.

Vora, Neha. *Impossible Citizens: Dubai's Indian Diaspora.* Durham: Duke University Press, 2013.

Weber, Max. "Science as a Vocation." In *From Max Weber: Essays in Sociology,* translated by H. H. Gerth and C. Wright Mills, 129–56. New York: Oxford University Press, 1946.

Wolf, Martin. "Will the Nation-State Survive Globalization?" *Foreign Affairs* 80 (2001): 178–90

Young, Michael. "Bronislaw Malinowski." In *International Dictionary of Anthropologists*, edited by Christopher Winters, 444–6. New York: Garland Publishing, 1991.

Zahra, Tara. *Kidnapped Souls: National Indifference and the Battle for Children in the Bohemian Lands, 1900–1948.* Ithaca: Cornell University Press, 2008.

THE MACAT LIBRARY
BY DISCIPLINE

AFRICANA STUDIES

Chinua Achebe's *An Image of Africa: Racism in Conrad's Heart of Darkness*
W. E. B. Du Bois's *The Souls of Black Folk*
Zora Neale Huston's *Characteristics of Negro Expression*
Martin Luther King Jr's *Why We Can't Wait*
Toni Morrison's *Playing in the Dark: Whiteness in the American Literary Imagination*

ANTHROPOLOGY

Arjun Appadurai's *Modernity at Large: Cultural Dimensions of Globalisation*
Philippe Ariès's *Centuries of Childhood*
Franz Boas's *Race, Language and Culture*
Kim Chan & Renée Mauborgne's *Blue Ocean Strategy*
Jared Diamond's *Guns, Germs & Steel: the Fate of Human Societies*
Jared Diamond's *Collapse: How Societies Choose to Fail or Survive*
E. E. Evans-Pritchard's *Witchcraft, Oracles and Magic Among the Azande*
James Ferguson's *The Anti-Politics Machine*
Clifford Geertz's *The Interpretation of Cultures*
David Graeber's *Debt: the First 5000 Years*
Karen Ho's *Liquidated: An Ethnography of Wall Street*
Geert Hofstede's *Culture's Consequences: Comparing Values, Behaviors, Institutes and Organizations across Nations*
Claude Lévi-Strauss's *Structural Anthropology*
Jay Macleod's *Ain't No Makin' It: Aspirations and Attainment in a Low-Income Neighborhood*
Saba Mahmood's *The Politics of Piety: The Islamic Revival and the Feminist Subject*
Marcel Mauss's *The Gift*

BUSINESS

Jean Lave & Etienne Wenger's *Situated Learning*
Theodore Levitt's *Marketing Myopia*
Burton G. Malkiel's *A Random Walk Down Wall Street*
Douglas McGregor's *The Human Side of Enterprise*
Michael Porter's *Competitive Strategy: Creating and Sustaining Superior Performance*
John Kotter's *Leading Change*
C. K. Prahalad & Gary Hamel's *The Core Competence of the Corporation*

CRIMINOLOGY

Michelle Alexander's *The New Jim Crow: Mass Incarceration in the Age of Colorblindness*
Michael R. Gottfredson & Travis Hirschi's *A General Theory of Crime*
Richard Herrnstein & Charles A. Murray's *The Bell Curve: Intelligence and Class Structure in American Life*
Elizabeth Loftus's *Eyewitness Testimony*
Jay Macleod's *Ain't No Makin' It: Aspirations and Attainment in a Low-Income Neighborhood*
Philip Zimbardo's *The Lucifer Effect*

ECONOMICS

Janet Abu-Lughod's *Before European Hegemony*
Ha-Joon Chang's *Kicking Away the Ladder*
David Brion Davis's *The Problem of Slavery in the Age of Revolution*
Milton Friedman's *The Role of Monetary Policy*
Milton Friedman's *Capitalism and Freedom*
David Graeber's *Debt: the First 5000 Years*
Friedrich Hayek's *The Road to Serfdom*
Karen Ho's *Liquidated: An Ethnography of Wall Street*

John Maynard Keynes's *The General Theory of Employment, Interest and Money*
Charles P. Kindleberger's *Manias, Panics and Crashes*
Robert Lucas's *Why Doesn't Capital Flow from Rich to Poor Countries?*
Burton G. Malkiel's *A Random Walk Down Wall Street*
Thomas Robert Malthus's *An Essay on the Principle of Population*
Karl Marx's *Capital*
Thomas Piketty's *Capital in the Twenty-First Century*
Amartya Sen's *Development as Freedom*
Adam Smith's *The Wealth of Nations*
Nassim Nicholas Taleb's *The Black Swan: The Impact of the Highly Improbable*
Amos Tversky's & Daniel Kahneman's *Judgment under Uncertainty: Heuristics and Biases*
Mahbub Ul Haq's *Reflections on Human Development*
Max Weber's *The Protestant Ethic and the Spirit of Capitalism*

FEMINISM AND GENDER STUDIES

Judith Butler's *Gender Trouble*
Simone De Beauvoir's *The Second Sex*
Michel Foucault's *History of Sexuality*
Betty Friedan's *The Feminine Mystique*
Saba Mahmood's *The Politics of Piety: The Islamic Revival and the Feminist Subject*
Joan Wallach Scott's *Gender and the Politics of History*
Mary Wollstonecraft's *A Vindication of the Rights of Woman*
Virginia Woolf's *A Room of One's Own*

GEOGRAPHY

The Brundtland Report's *Our Common Future*
Rachel Carson's *Silent Spring*
Charles Darwin's *On the Origin of Species*
James Ferguson's *The Anti-Politics Machine*
Jane Jacobs's *The Death and Life of Great American Cities*
James Lovelock's *Gaia: A New Look at Life on Earth*
Amartya Sen's *Development as Freedom*
Mathis Wackernagel & William Rees's *Our Ecological Footprint*

HISTORY

Janet Abu-Lughod's *Before European Hegemony*
Benedict Anderson's *Imagined Communities*
Bernard Bailyn's *The Ideological Origins of the American Revolution*
Hanna Batatu's *The Old Social Classes And The Revolutionary Movements Of Iraq*
Christopher Browning's *Ordinary Men: Reserve Police Batallion 101 and the Final Solution in Poland*
Edmund Burke's *Reflections on the Revolution in France*
William Cronon's *Nature's Metropolis: Chicago And The Great West*
Alfred W. Crosby's *The Columbian Exchange*
Hamid Dabashi's *Iran: A People Interrupted*
David Brion Davis's *The Problem of Slavery in the Age of Revolution*
Nathalie Zemon Davis's *The Return of Martin Guerre*
Jared Diamond's *Guns, Germs & Steel: the Fate of Human Societies*
Frank Dikotter's *Mao's Great Famine*
John W Dower's *War Without Mercy: Race And Power In The Pacific War*
W. E. B. Du Bois's *The Souls of Black Folk*
Richard J. Evans's *In Defence of History*
Lucien Febvre's *The Problem of Unbelief in the 16th Century*
Sheila Fitzpatrick's *Everyday Stalinism*

The Macat Library By Discipline

Eric Foner's *Reconstruction: America's Unfinished Revolution, 1863-1877*
Michel Foucault's *Discipline and Punish*
Michel Foucault's *History of Sexuality*
Francis Fukuyama's *The End of History and the Last Man*
John Lewis Gaddis's *We Now Know: Rethinking Cold War History*
Ernest Gellner's *Nations and Nationalism*
Eugene Genovese's *Roll, Jordan, Roll: The World the Slaves Made*
Carlo Ginzburg's *The Night Battles*
Daniel Goldhagen's *Hitler's Willing Executioners*
Jack Goldstone's *Revolution and Rebellion in the Early Modern World*
Antonio Gramsci's *The Prison Notebooks*
Alexander Hamilton, John Jay & James Madison's *The Federalist Papers*
Christopher Hill's *The World Turned Upside Down*
Carole Hillenbrand's *The Crusades: Islamic Perspectives*
Thomas Hobbes's *Leviathan*
Eric Hobsbawm's *The Age Of Revolution*
John A. Hobson's *Imperialism: A Study*
Albert Hourani's *History of the Arab Peoples*
Samuel P. Huntington's *The Clash of Civilizations and the Remaking of World Order*
C. L. R. James's *The Black Jacobins*
Tony Judt's *Postwar: A History of Europe Since 1945*
Ernst Kantorowicz's *The King's Two Bodies: A Study in Medieval Political Theology*
Paul Kennedy's *The Rise and Fall of the Great Powers*
Ian Kershaw's *The "Hitler Myth": Image and Reality in the Third Reich*
John Maynard Keynes's *The General Theory of Employment, Interest and Money*
Charles P. Kindleberger's *Manias, Panics and Crashes*
Martin Luther King Jr's *Why We Can't Wait*
Henry Kissinger's *World Order: Reflections on the Character of Nations and the Course of History*
Thomas Kuhn's *The Structure of Scientific Revolutions*
Georges Lefebvre's *The Coming of the French Revolution*
John Locke's *Two Treatises of Government*
Niccolò Machiavelli's *The Prince*
Thomas Robert Malthus's *An Essay on the Principle of Population*
Mahmood Mamdani's *Citizen and Subject: Contemporary Africa And The Legacy Of Late Colonialism*
Karl Marx's *Capital*
Stanley Milgram's *Obedience to Authority*
John Stuart Mill's *On Liberty*
Thomas Paine's *Common Sense*
Thomas Paine's *Rights of Man*
Geoffrey Parker's *Global Crisis: War, Climate Change and Catastrophe in the Seventeenth Century*
Jonathan Riley-Smith's *The First Crusade and the Idea of Crusading*
Jean-Jacques Rousseau's *The Social Contract*
Joan Wallach Scott's *Gender and the Politics of History*
Theda Skocpol's *States and Social Revolutions*
Adam Smith's *The Wealth of Nations*
Timothy Snyder's *Bloodlands: Europe Between Hitler and Stalin*
Sun Tzu's *The Art of War*
Keith Thomas's *Religion and the Decline of Magic*
Thucydides's *The History of the Peloponnesian War*
Frederick Jackson Turner's *The Significance of the Frontier in American History*
Odd Arne Westad's *The Global Cold War: Third World Interventions And The Making Of Our Times*

LITERATURE

Chinua Achebe's *An Image of Africa: Racism in Conrad's Heart of Darkness*
Roland Barthes's *Mythologies*
Homi K. Bhabha's *The Location of Culture*
Judith Butler's *Gender Trouble*
Simone De Beauvoir's *The Second Sex*
Ferdinand De Saussure's *Course in General Linguistics*
T. S. Eliot's *The Sacred Wood: Essays on Poetry and Criticism*
Zora Neale Huston's *Characteristics of Negro Expression*
Toni Morrison's *Playing in the Dark: Whiteness in the American Literary Imagination*
Edward Said's *Orientalism*
Gayatri Chakravorty Spivak's *Can the Subaltern Speak?*
Mary Wollstonecraft's *A Vindication of the Rights of Women*
Virginia Woolf's *A Room of One's Own*

PHILOSOPHY

Elizabeth Anscombe's *Modern Moral Philosophy*
Hannah Arendt's *The Human Condition*
Aristotle's *Metaphysics*
Aristotle's *Nicomachean Ethics*
Edmund Gettier's *Is Justified True Belief Knowledge?*
Georg Wilhelm Friedrich Hegel's *Phenomenology of Spirit*
David Hume's *Dialogues Concerning Natural Religion*
David Hume's *The Enquiry for Human Understanding*
Immanuel Kant's *Religion within the Boundaries of Mere Reason*
Immanuel Kant's *Critique of Pure Reason*
Søren Kierkegaard's *The Sickness Unto Death*
Søren Kierkegaard's *Fear and Trembling*
C. S. Lewis's *The Abolition of Man*
Alasdair MacIntyre's *After Virtue*
Marcus Aurelius's *Meditations*
Friedrich Nietzsche's *On the Genealogy of Morality*
Friedrich Nietzsche's *Beyond Good and Evil*
Plato's *Republic*
Plato's *Symposium*
Jean-Jacques Rousseau's *The Social Contract*
Gilbert Ryle's *The Concept of Mind*
Baruch Spinoza's *Ethics*
Sun Tzu's *The Art of War*
Ludwig Wittgenstein's *Philosophical Investigations*

POLITICS

Benedict Anderson's *Imagined Communities*
Aristotle's *Politics*
Bernard Bailyn's *The Ideological Origins of the American Revolution*
Edmund Burke's *Reflections on the Revolution in France*
John C. Calhoun's *A Disquisition on Government*
Ha-Joon Chang's *Kicking Away the Ladder*
Hamid Dabashi's *Iran: A People Interrupted*
Hamid Dabashi's *Theology of Discontent: The Ideological Foundation of the Islamic Revolution in Iran*
Robert Dahl's *Democracy and its Critics*
Robert Dahl's *Who Governs?*
David Brion Davis's *The Problem of Slavery in the Age of Revolution*

The Macat Library By Discipline

Alexis De Tocqueville's *Democracy in America*
James Ferguson's *The Anti-Politics Machine*
Frank Dikotter's *Mao's Great Famine*
Sheila Fitzpatrick's *Everyday Stalinism*
Eric Foner's *Reconstruction: America's Unfinished Revolution, 1863-1877*
Milton Friedman's *Capitalism and Freedom*
Francis Fukuyama's *The End of History and the Last Man*
John Lewis Gaddis's *We Now Know: Rethinking Cold War History*
Ernest Gellner's *Nations and Nationalism*
David Graeber's *Debt: the First 5000 Years*
Antonio Gramsci's *The Prison Notebooks*
Alexander Hamilton, John Jay & James Madison's *The Federalist Papers*
Friedrich Hayek's *The Road to Serfdom*
Christopher Hill's *The World Turned Upside Down*
Thomas Hobbes's *Leviathan*
John A. Hobson's *Imperialism: A Study*
Samuel P. Huntington's *The Clash of Civilizations and the Remaking of World Order*
Tony Judt's *Postwar: A History of Europe Since 1945*
David C. Kang's *China Rising: Peace, Power and Order in East Asia*
Paul Kennedy's *The Rise and Fall of Great Powers*
Robert Keohane's *After Hegemony*
Martin Luther King Jr.'s *Why We Can't Wait*
Henry Kissinger's *World Order: Reflections on the Character of Nations and the Course of History*
John Locke's *Two Treatises of Government*
Niccolò Machiavelli's *The Prince*
Thomas Robert Malthus's *An Essay on the Principle of Population*
Mahmood Mamdani's *Citizen and Subject: Contemporary Africa And The Legacy Of Late Colonialism*
Karl Marx's *Capital*
John Stuart Mill's *On Liberty*
John Stuart Mill's *Utilitarianism*
Hans Morgenthau's *Politics Among Nations*
Thomas Paine's *Common Sense*
Thomas Paine's *Rights of Man*
Thomas Piketty's *Capital in the Twenty-First Century*
Robert D. Putman's *Bowling Alone*
John Rawls's *Theory of Justice*
Jean-Jacques Rousseau's *The Social Contract*
Theda Skocpol's *States and Social Revolutions*
Adam Smith's *The Wealth of Nations*
Sun Tzu's *The Art of War*
Henry David Thoreau's *Civil Disobedience*
Thucydides's *The History of the Peloponnesian War*
Kenneth Waltz's *Theory of International Politics*
Max Weber's *Politics as a Vocation*
Odd Arne Westad's *The Global Cold War: Third World Interventions And The Making Of Our Times*

POSTCOLONIAL STUDIES

Roland Barthes's *Mythologies*
Frantz Fanon's *Black Skin, White Masks*
Homi K. Bhabha's *The Location of Culture*
Gustavo Gutiérrez's *A Theology of Liberation*
Edward Said's *Orientalism*
Gayatri Chakravorty Spivak's *Can the Subaltern Speak?*

PSYCHOLOGY

Gordon Allport's *The Nature of Prejudice*
Alan Baddeley & Graham Hitch's *Aggression: A Social Learning Analysis*
Albert Bandura's *Aggression: A Social Learning Analysis*
Leon Festinger's *A Theory of Cognitive Dissonance*
Sigmund Freud's *The Interpretation of Dreams*
Betty Friedan's *The Feminine Mystique*
Michael R. Gottfredson & Travis Hirschi's *A General Theory of Crime*
Eric Hoffer's *The True Believer: Thoughts on the Nature of Mass Movements*
William James's *Principles of Psychology*
Elizabeth Loftus's *Eyewitness Testimony*
A. H. Maslow's *A Theory of Human Motivation*
Stanley Milgram's *Obedience to Authority*
Steven Pinker's *The Better Angels of Our Nature*
Oliver Sacks's *The Man Who Mistook His Wife For a Hat*
Richard Thaler & Cass Sunstein's *Nudge: Improving Decisions About Health, Wealth and Happiness*
Amos Tversky's *Judgment under Uncertainty: Heuristics and Biases*
Philip Zimbardo's *The Lucifer Effect*

SCIENCE

Rachel Carson's *Silent Spring*
William Cronon's *Nature's Metropolis: Chicago And The Great West*
Alfred W. Crosby's *The Columbian Exchange*
Charles Darwin's *On the Origin of Species*
Richard Dawkin's *The Selfish Gene*
Thomas Kuhn's *The Structure of Scientific Revolutions*
Geoffrey Parker's *Global Crisis: War, Climate Change and Catastrophe in the Seventeenth Century*
Mathis Wackernagel & William Rees's *Our Ecological Footprint*

SOCIOLOGY

Michelle Alexander's *The New Jim Crow: Mass Incarceration in the Age of Colorblindness*
Gordon Allport's *The Nature of Prejudice*
Albert Bandura's *Aggression: A Social Learning Analysis*
Hanna Batatu's *The Old Social Classes And The Revolutionary Movements Of Iraq*
Ha-Joon Chang's *Kicking Away the Ladder*
W. E. B. Du Bois's *The Souls of Black Folk*
Émile Durkheim's *On Suicide*
Frantz Fanon's *Black Skin, White Masks*
Frantz Fanon's *The Wretched of the Earth*
Eric Foner's *Reconstruction: America's Unfinished Revolution, 1863-1877*
Eugene Genovese's *Roll, Jordan, Roll: The World the Slaves Made*
Jack Goldstone's *Revolution and Rebellion in the Early Modern World*
Antonio Gramsci's *The Prison Notebooks*
Richard Herrnstein & Charles A Murray's *The Bell Curve: Intelligence and Class Structure in American Life*
Eric Hoffer's *The True Believer: Thoughts on the Nature of Mass Movements*
Jane Jacobs's *The Death and Life of Great American Cities*
Robert Lucas's *Why Doesn't Capital Flow from Rich to Poor Countries?*
Jay Macleod's *Ain't No Makin' It: Aspirations and Attainment in a Low Income Neighborhood*
Elaine May's *Homeward Bound: American Families in the Cold War Era*
Douglas McGregor's *The Human Side of Enterprise*
C. Wright Mills's *The Sociological Imagination*

The Macat Library By Discipline

Thomas Piketty's *Capital in the Twenty-First Century*
Robert D. Putman's *Bowling Alone*
David Riesman's *The Lonely Crowd: A Study of the Changing American Character*
Edward Said's *Orientalism*
Joan Wallach Scott's *Gender and the Politics of History*
Theda Skocpol's *States and Social Revolutions*
Max Weber's *The Protestant Ethic and the Spirit of Capitalism*

THEOLOGY

Augustine's *Confessions*
Benedict's *Rule of St Benedict*
Gustavo Gutiérrez's *A Theology of Liberation*
Carole Hillenbrand's *The Crusades: Islamic Perspectives*
David Hume's *Dialogues Concerning Natural Religion*
Immanuel Kant's *Religion within the Boundaries of Mere Reason*
Ernst Kantorowicz's *The King's Two Bodies: A Study in Medieval Political Theology*
Søren Kierkegaard's *The Sickness Unto Death*
C. S. Lewis's *The Abolition of Man*
Saba Mahmood's *The Politics of Piety: The Islamic Revival and the Feminist Subject*
Baruch Spinoza's *Ethics*
Keith Thomas's *Religion and the Decline of Magic*

COMING SOON

Chris Argyris's *The Individual and the Organisation*
Seyla Benhabib's *The Rights of Others*
Walter Benjamin's *The Work Of Art in the Age of Mechanical Reproduction*
John Berger's *Ways of Seeing*
Pierre Bourdieu's *Outline of a Theory of Practice*
Mary Douglas's *Purity and Danger*
Roland Dworkin's *Taking Rights Seriously*
James G. March's *Exploration and Exploitation in Organisational Learning*
Ikujiro Nonaka's *A Dynamic Theory of Organizational Knowledge Creation*
Griselda Pollock's *Vision and Difference*
Amartya Sen's *Inequality Re-Examined*
Susan Sontag's *On Photography*
Yasser Tabbaa's *The Transformation of Islamic Art*
Ludwig von Mises's *Theory of Money and Credit*

Macat Disciplines

Access the greatest ideas and thinkers across entire disciplines, including

Postcolonial Studies

Roland Barthes's *Mythologies*
Frantz Fanon's *Black Skin, White Masks*
Homi K. Bhabha's *The Location of Culture*
Gustavo Gutiérrez's *A Theology of Liberation*
Edward Said's *Orientalism*
Gayatri Chakravorty Spivak's *Can the Subaltern Speak?*

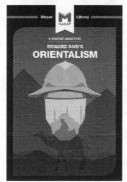

Macat analyses are available from all good bookshops and libraries.

Access hundreds of analyses through one, multimedia tool.
Join free for one month **library.macat.com**

Macat Disciplines

Access the greatest ideas and thinkers across entire disciplines, including

AFRICANA STUDIES

Chinua Achebe's *An Image of Africa: Racism in Conrad's Heart of Darkness*

W. E. B. Du Bois's *The Souls of Black Folk*

Zora Neale Hurston's *Characteristics of Negro Expression*

Martin Luther King Jr.'s *Why We Can't Wait*

Toni Morrison's *Playing in the Dark: Whiteness in the American Literary Imagination*

Macat Disciplines

Access the greatest ideas and thinkers across entire disciplines, including

FEMINISM, GENDER AND QUEER STUDIES

Simone De Beauvoir's
The Second Sex

Michel Foucault's
History of Sexuality

Betty Friedan's
The Feminine Mystique

Saba Mahmood's
*The Politics of Piety:
The Islamic Revival and
the Feminist Subject*

Joan Wallach Scott's
*Gender and the
Politics of History*

Mary Wollstonecraft's
*A Vindication of the
Rights of Woman*

Virginia Woolf's
A Room of One's Own

Judith Butler's
Gender Trouble

Macat Disciplines

Access the greatest ideas and thinkers across entire disciplines, including

CRIMINOLOGY

Michelle Alexander's
The New Jim Crow: Mass Incarceration in the Age of Colorblindness

Michael R. Gottfredson & Travis Hirschi's
A General Theory of Crime

Elizabeth Loftus's
Eyewitness Testimony

Richard Herrnstein & Charles A. Murray's
The Bell Curve: Intelligence and Class Structure in American Life

Jay Macleod's
Ain't No Makin' It: Aspirations and Attainment in a Low-Income Neighborhood

Philip Zimbardo's
The Lucifer Effect

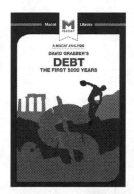

Macat Disciplines

Access the greatest ideas and thinkers across entire disciplines, including

GLOBALIZATION

Arjun Appadurai's, *Modernity at Large: Cultural Dimensions of Globalisation*

James Ferguson's, *The Anti-Politics Machine*

Geert Hofstede's, *Culture's Consequences*

Amartya Sen's, *Development as Freedom*

Macat Disciplines

Access the greatest ideas and thinkers across entire disciplines, including

MAN AND THE ENVIRONMENT

The Brundtland Report's, *Our Common Future*
Rachel Carson's, *Silent Spring*
James Lovelock's, *Gaia: A New Look at Life on Earth*
Mathis Wackernagel & William Rees's, *Our Ecological Footprint*

Macat analyses are available from all good bookshops and libraries.

Access hundreds of analyses through one, multimedia tool.
Join free for one month **library.macat.com**

Macat Disciplines

Access the greatest ideas and thinkers across entire disciplines, including

TOTALITARIANISM

Sheila Fitzpatrick's, *Everyday Stalinism*
Ian Kershaw's, *The "Hitler Myth"*
Timothy Snyder's, *Bloodlands*

Macat Pairs

Analyse historical and modern issues from opposite sides of an argument. Pairs include:

RACE AND IDENTITY

Zora Neale Hurston's
Characteristics of Negro Expression

Using material collected on anthropological expeditions to the South, Zora Neale Hurston explains how expression in African American culture in the early twentieth century departs from the art of white America. At the time, African American art was often criticized for copying white culture. For Hurston, this criticism misunderstood how art works. European tradition views art as something fixed. But Hurston describes a creative process that is alive, ever-changing, and largely improvisational. She maintains that African American art works through a process called 'mimicry'—where an imitated object or verbal pattern, for example, is reshaped and altered until it becomes something new, novel—and worthy of attention.

Frantz Fanon's
Black Skin, White Masks

Black Skin, White Masks offers a radical analysis of the psychological effects of colonization on the colonized.

Fanon witnessed the effects of colonization first hand both in his birthplace, Martinique, and again later in life when he worked as a psychiatrist in another French colony, Algeria. His text is uncompromising in form and argument. He dissects the dehumanizing effects of colonialism, arguing that it destroys the native sense of identity, forcing people to adapt to an alien set of values—including a core belief that they are inferior. This results in deep psychological trauma.

Fanon's work played a pivotal role in the civil rights movements of the 1960s.

Macat analyses are available from all good bookshops and libraries.

Access hundreds of analyses through one, multimedia tool.
Join free for one month **library.macat.com**

Macat Pairs

Analyse historical and modern issues from opposite sides of an argument. Pairs include:

INTERNATIONAL RELATIONS IN THE 21ST CENTURY

Samuel P. Huntington's
The Clash of Civilisations

In his highly influential 1996 book, Huntington offers a vision of a post-Cold War world in which conflict takes place not between competing ideologies but between cultures. The worst clash, he argues, will be between the Islamic world and the West: the West's arrogance and belief that its culture is a "gift" to the world will come into conflict with Islam's obstinacy and concern that its culture is under attack from a morally decadent "other."

Clash inspired much debate between different political schools of thought. But its greatest impact came in helping define American foreign policy in the wake of the 2001 terrorist attacks in New York and Washington.

Francis Fukuyama's
The End of History and the Last Man

Published in 1992, *The End of History and the Last Man* argues that capitalist democracy is the final destination for all societies. Fukuyama believed democracy triumphed during the Cold War because it lacks the "fundamental contradictions" inherent in communism and satisfies our yearning for freedom and equality. Democracy therefore marks the endpoint in the evolution of ideology, and so the "end of history." There will still be "events," but no fundamental change in ideology.

Macat Pairs

Analyse historical and modern issues from opposite sides of an argument. Pairs include:

HOW TO RUN AN ECONOMY

John Maynard Keynes's
The General Theory OF Employment, Interest and Money

Classical economics suggests that market economies are self-correcting in times of recession or depression, and tend toward full employment and output. But English economist John Maynard Keynes disagrees.

In his ground-breaking 1936 study *The General Theory*, Keynes argues that traditional economics has misunderstood the causes of unemployment. Employment is not determined by the price of labor; it is directly linked to demand. Keynes believes market economies are by nature unstable, and so require government intervention. Spurred on by the social catastrophe of the Great Depression of the 1930s, he sets out to revolutionize the way the world thinks

Milton Friedman's
The Role of Monetary Policy

Friedman's 1968 paper changed the course of economic theory. In just 17 pages, he demolished existing theory and outlined an effective alternate monetary policy designed to secure 'high employment, stable prices and rapid growth.'

Friedman demonstrated that monetary policy plays a vital role in broader economic stability and argued that economists got their monetary policy wrong in the 1950s and 1960s by misunderstanding the relationship between inflation and unemployment. Previous generations of economists had believed that governments could permanently decrease unemployment by permitting inflation—and vice versa. Friedman's most original contribution was to show that this supposed trade-off is an illusion that only works in the short term.

Macat analyses are available from all good bookshops and libraries.

Access hundreds of analyses through one, multimedia tool.
Join free for one month **library.macat.com**

Macat Pairs

Analyse historical and modern issues from opposite sides of an argument. Pairs include:

ARE WE FUNDAMENTALLY GOOD - OR BAD?

Steven Pinker's
The Better Angels of Our Nature

Stephen Pinker's gloriously optimistic 2011 book argues that, despite humanity's biological tendency toward violence, we are, in fact, less violent today than ever before. To prove his case, Pinker lays out pages of detailed statistical evidence. For him, much of the credit for the decline goes to the eighteenth-century Enlightenment movement, whose ideas of liberty, tolerance, and respect for the value of human life filtered down through society and affected how people thought. That psychological change led to behavioral change—and overall we became more peaceful. Critics countered that humanity could never overcome the biological urge toward violence; others argued that Pinker's statistics were flawed.

Philip Zimbardo's
The Lucifer Effect

Some psychologists believe those who commit cruelty are innately evil. Zimbardo disagrees. In *The Lucifer Effect*, he argues that sometimes good people do evil things simply because of the situations they find themselves in, citing many historical examples to illustrate his point. Zimbardo details his 1971 Stanford prison experiment, where ordinary volunteers playing guards in a mock prison rapidly became abusive. But he also describes the tortures committed by US army personnel in Iraq's Abu Ghraib prison in 2003—and how he himself testified in defence of one of those guards. committed by US army personnel in Iraq's Abu Ghraib prison in 2003—and how he himself testified in defence of one of those guards.

Macat Pairs

Analyse historical and modern issues from opposite sides of an argument. Pairs include:

HOW WE RELATE TO EACH OTHER AND SOCIETY

Jean-Jacques Rousseau's
The Social Contract

Rousseau's famous work sets out the radical concept of the 'social contract': a give-and-take relationship between individual freedom and social order.

If people are free to do as they like, governed only by their own sense of justice, they are also vulnerable to chaos and violence. To avoid this, Rousseau proposes, they should agree to give up some freedom to benefit from the protection of social and political organization. But this deal is only just if societies are led by the collective needs and desires of the people, and able to control the private interests of individuals. For Rousseau, the only legitimate form of government is rule by the people.

Robert D. Putnam's
Bowling Alone

In *Bowling Alone*, Robert Putnam argues that Americans have become disconnected from one another and from the institutions of their common life, and investigates the consequences of this change.

Looking at a range of indicators, from membership in formal organizations to the number of invitations being extended to informal dinner parties, Putnam demonstrates that Americans are interacting less and creating less "social capital" – with potentially disastrous implications for their society.

It would be difficult to overstate the impact of *Bowling Alone*, one of the most frequently cited social science publications of the last half-century.

Macat analyses are available from all good bookshops and libraries.

Access hundreds of analyses through one, multimedia tool.
Join free for one month **library.macat.com**

Printed in the United States
by Baker & Taylor Publisher Services